In our hurried, distracted, careless and materialistic age, it is the beginning of wisdom to slow down and attend the world around us, to see anew the natural cycles and splendors, to experience time without rush or fear, to connect with the things of our planet, with others, and with the past, beyond ego and greed, to understand the spirituality of the daily, the extraordinary in the ordinary, to be at home in your own life. This is what Fred Waage does in SINKING CREEK JOURNAL.

—Robert Morgan, Author of *The Strange Attractor: New and Selected Poems*

This beautiful and unique Book of Days kept me reading well past my bedtime for several nights running. In sensuous prose that borders on poetry, Frederick Waage records the intricate interactions among the creatures and plants, the weather and water and rocks, around the land on which he lives. As I read, this land itself stirred to life like a character in a crime novel, with many varied pursuers. Sinking Creek, Tennessee, became for me a microcosm of our endangered globe, and I started looking at my own surroundings with more attention, appreciation—and concern. With SINKING CREEK JOURNAL Waage joins the ranks of our great nature writers like Annie Dillard and Lewis Thomas, from whom he quotes so effectively in his own writing.

—Lisa Alther, Author of *Kinflicks*

SINKING CREEK JOURNAL
An Environmental Book of Days

Fred Waage

Little Creek Books

A division of Mountain Girl Press
Bristol, VA

A division of Mountain Girl Press
Bristol, VA

Sinking Creek Journal
An Environmental Book of Days

Published May 2010
All rights reserved.

Copyright © 2010
Cover and interior design by Carlson ProType

This book may not be reproduced in whole or part, in any matter whatsoever without written permission, with the exception of brief quotations within book reviews or articles.

You may contact the publisher at:
Little Creek Books
An imprint of Mountain Girl Press
P.O. Box 17013
Bristol, VA 24209-7013
E-mail: publisher@littlecreekbooks.com

ISBN: 978-0-9843192-2-0

Letter to the Reader

Welcome to Sinking Creek, the only trout stream inside the civic boundaries of Johnson City, Tennessee. Although it makes excursions elsewhere, the stream and foothills above it are the main sites for this daily chronicle of a solar year in the Southern Appalachians.

As the author, I hope that you will consider this as a "daybook" in the true usage of the term: as a book of daily readings from the gospel of nature, which can be a companion volume for you in your own daily living on our threatened earth.

I have tried to shape these readings to be both informal and informative, and hope that you will experience them as nature's experiences more than the author's in nature. If the plants and creatures named in it could have written the text, I would have let them speak for themselves, but I am as you are, a prisoner of human language.

While wanting nature to speak for itself through me, I have to admit to a paradox: you will find here strong opinions, and anguished questions, cloaked by leaves, about the destructive role humans have played, are playing, and will continue to play, in the destruction of nature and that part of nature that is they themselves.

So it is my hope that, as well as a companion in your lives, *Sinking Creek Journal* may be an instigator of, if not action for, at least deep reflection on, what humans can do to reverse the damage they have wrought on the living world.

Fred Waage

The author wishes to acknowledge the valuable botanical advice of Dr. Tim McDowell, and the aid of many Association for the Study of Literature and Environment members in dating events of environmental importance.

Dedicated to:

Leif

Faye

semper fi

In memoriam:

Branna

Ki

Tam Lin

SINKING CREEK JOURNAL
An Environmental Book of Days

> [Its] beauty shall in these black lines be seen,
> And they shall live, and [it] in them still green.
> —Shakespeare, Sonnet 63 (amended)

September 23   **A SCARF OF SPARKS**

    High wind in a valley, between storms, piles the maple leaves (both green and brown) in eastward-rising clumps against porch rails. Single treed acre tosses tops a dozen different directions of gust. Trailing uphill with collies, 8 AM, dry hardwood forest provides only specious shelter. Pileated woodpecker cries inside vague distant tree-roar. Below, white asters' petals—yellow, though blue-stemmed goldenrod (*solidago caesia*) remains strong. Friend Susan has bought seven acres out on Cherokee Road, holds a property-warming. Her camper is set on a high knob beside a buzzing yellowjacket maw. Warm wind relentlessly waves tarp, grillsmoke, convergent voices. From bonfire, a scarf of sparks flares out against dark trees.

> " . . . *our methods of order . . . imitate an order which is indefinitely resourceful . . . It is like this September evening after rain. For a short time . . . not long before dark, the earth is colored with magic, shadowless light . . . All colors are sure and strong, joining in pure gradations. The evening is full of mystic peace.*" John Hay, **Nature's Year**, 1961

Sinking Creek Journal

September 24   **VULTURES**

Returning from newspaper box, early morning, kettle of vultures stirred above mountainside. Ours are mostly grey vultures; few tilted yesterday's winds, nothing like the flotillas a few years ago, perched, weighing tulip poplar branches, flapping heavily, leering at the border collies; vultures, who cleanse the earth, give evidence that there are many neighborhood creatures available to be squashed, and many more vehicles available to squash them. Raindrops teem, glint burned-out hibiscus leaves. Foreign grosbeaks in the dogwoods—a pair so contrasting, male flashes rosy breast and white wing bars, brown-streaked female, all one tone. Three yard dogwoods, each at different yellowing stage, but berries of all three flash enticement—the yard's red light district.

*1906—Teddy Roosevelt creates Devil's Tower
as U.S.'s first national monument*

September 25   **HIBISCUS**

Useless to deny grey clouds, chill air, despite neighbors' attempts to reheat affect with mowers, blowers, trimmers. Few leaves have degreened, but felt is their drooping, dusty resignation. The jolly braided hibiscus should be long gone, yet one more pink bud has boomed, wide as a cup, O'Keefian; its protruberant stamen, sensitive extrusions, are shimmers of heat solidified. This is great red hibiscus (*hibiscus coccineus*), a Southeastern native, grown by Bartram, Washington, Jefferson, in whose reconstituted garden this particular individual grew up. Some design of genetics, soil, temperature, has made this one flower defy the time—if design govern in a thing so small.

1893—Sequoia National Park established

September 26   **FARMSTEAD**

Mountain mist, mist over stream, temperature 46. Above the dump, above the murder of crows, where wooded rise peaks, to fall away and rise again as Buffalo Mountain, the Bastian family farmed for decades. In the

1980s, cattle still foraged this second-growth woodland. Then, the clearing where the farmhouse had presumably been, surviving domestics held out—boxwood, yucca, ornamentals; aged-out apple trees' twisted trunks scaled out, still alive. Until recently all this once-humanized space was growing back, vines covered appletree corpses, cross on the Bastians' burial vault disarmed by fallen limbs. Now wide cartways have been cleared where farmpaths were and were not. Cleared brush mounded, treadmarks appear and are washed out, over and over. Turkey corn strewn here. Why these openings? Why this reversion to human use?

"The old appletree was dead and lay prostrate across the graves, but from the base of the rotting trunk there sprang a few wiry shoots, still living." Louis Bromfield, **The Farm**, 1933

September 27   **INSECTS**

6:00 PM: sun in pine cleft just about reaching treeline of the hill across Sinking Creek valley. Angled so, it sparks insects beyond number, they twinkle, foregrounding dark treewall. Through needles, sun is fanned, webbed, entangled. Two mowers putter to a pop. How can there be so much life in the air? Like the harsh fallen ragweed stems, uprooted, encasing the uprooter in a pollen glitterball, recalling puffball spores released by tromp of pre-pubescent feet. And Lewis Thomas on the perpetual insect-fall we do not see, natural death rain from a mile above. It takes a slant of light to reveal the human insignificance amid this infinitesimal teeming glory. Now a door slams and a dozen mourning doves explode upward like shrapnel from an IED.

1962—Rachel Carson's **Silent Spring** *released*

September 28,
Staunton VA   **MOUNTED MOOSE**

Texas Roadhouse—bearhead and moosehead (are there moose in Texas?) protrude so far from the wall that any seven-foot cowpoke could suffer a concussion sitting down to consume his sea onion. No one in the Virginia Texas Roadhouse wears a cowboy hat except one extremely ancient dude, maybe a real Texan crippled in a corral shootout. A couple of friends, one black, one white, change seats to place themselves directly beneath the droolless muzzle of the mounted moose. Watching them there, greeting friends, barbecue sauce of din lapping over them, one feels male *homo sapiens* of all races and creeds can find unity and harmony under the aegis of one common interest—the killing of large mammals (not excluding their own species).

1976— Congress passes Federal Land Policy Management Act

September 29,
Piscataway NJ   **SURVIVOR**

How intensely do inter-human concerns ignore the physical world humans must live in? How intensely must they do so? He died in March, his friends and neighbors officiously cleared and mowed his yard, removed the windfalls and dying trees. How empty hangs the bird feeder, how overgrown his small tomato patch! How bravely unfurls his U.S. flag in front! This is his survivor's place, and we will not allow her to be deprived of it. His ships and barometer remain on the walls. Her birds and squirrels no longer visit, however; her outdoors is too clean, deer that used to ply her overgrowth now visit the verdure across the street. Horror of the built environment grows, yet as its child you cannot disown it without losing all that makes the human One.

"Combining the force of its various units, our culture pushed itself like the web of the tent caterpillar across the face of nature."
Harvey Broome, **Out Under the Sky of the Great Smokies**, 1975

September 30,
Piscataway (Stelton), NJ   **TURKEYS**

Most is still green while premonitory rain-pricked wind scatters yellow elm-leaves between strip malls. Like lingering leaves, a few sunken storefronts and single-storied plaster houses—walls embossed with Heroic

Workers of the World—clutch condo-demned streets to testify Stelton's history as a wild Redfoul refuge. Today only the sumac is red. For old time's sake, cruising the flat overtaken land, where herring gulls land on the WalMart parking lot, grey, disembodied horses graze a holdout pasture between Rosebud Road and Coventry Close. Zirkel Avenue's branches embraced scalped land a few years ago, but the thousand boxes foreseen did not bloom there; inexplicable overgrown field persists. A sudden brake: wild turkey flock crossing the road, gobbling about politics. Wild turkeys, feeling entitled, not one wing is spread. A few houses down, neighborhood kids ride bikes and toss hoops, cul-de-sac. Now the turkeys are crossing the other direction, back towards the houses, with blatant air of unconcern commuting between the best of two worlds.

1882—world's first hydroelectric plant opens, Appleton, Wisconsin

October 1,
Tarrytown, NY **MOTH-SHAPED SAILS**

Blackbirds flock, Castle gates loom. Approaching battlements, a deer park opens out and closes in. The Castle is grey, built, they say, for Justice John Jay. Rains have lifted. White snakeroots lights every dark hedgerow. From a veranda corner, Tappan Zee bridge is visible, humming far off . . . blue water, moth-shaped sails. Wedding arch, fake flowers, string quartet. All the celebrants seem to be dressed in black. Downslope toward the sunset. Justice Jay must have had a dock below his castle on the Hudson. Now the Hudson is fenced and railed off: four Amtrak lines. Sun sinks into Catskill clouds as trains roar by. Climbing the slope, meet Melissa and Ben heading down, gin and tonics in hand. "This is so gatsbyesque!" she exclaims. But we row futilely against such tides. Some of us preserve our illusions so our illusions will preserve us.

"Over the course of centuries and scores of centuries, the river would writhe slowly but continuously across the floodplain, making its way in moving coils and loops, smoothing sand and earth the way an eel would, if you put an eel on a beach, and let him squirm back to the sea."
Franklin Burroughs, **The River Home** (1992)

Sinking Creek Journal

October 2,
Shippensburg, PA   **WILD FIELDS**

Afternoon

Wild fields behind lawns, storefronts, behind adult structures, summon. Intense October light slants. White asters with yellow centers, goldenrod brooms . . . leading far back to the treeline of memories. Dead spikes of yarrowlike cactus, thistledown outbursts, sumac oases, trodden rabbit, chipmunk tunnels: surely as complex a highway system back under these flowers as the Interstate itself. Bee on every flowerhead, one monarch over it all.

Night

Orange lights far away. On the two yards of groomed grass preceding the wild field, widespread rabbit community scatters into tangle of organic safety. Tail whites flash up the instant before flight. Low locust buzz. Chantry of resignation and call to endure. Orange lights deny a whole realm of change.

Morning

Light mist, still flowers, no bee stirs. Rain has just passed. Torn clouds heading east mirrored in oilsheen. No breeze on earth. The creation awaits.

1968—*Wild and Scenic Rivers Act passed*

October 3   **FAMILIAR PLACE**

Resuming a familiar place after a short absence: millions of cells shed, countless insects dead, chemical reactions have ravaged molecules, but sun still sets behind pines in relatively the same place, border collie lurks behind same birdbath to chase same tennis ball, same flies dive into same red wine. You are felled only by too much observation. There were no fallen pin oak leaves before. Virginia creeper leaves were red before. Before, a last flowering cultivar—pineapple sage—had not thrust forth its vermillion sabres. No large brown toad on the back porch. It is a warm evening for October. Voices lurch the valley down, brazen chipmunk and timorous dove break seeds together.

Fred Waage

World Habitat Day

October 4,
Columbia SC   **RESTORATION**

Fallen by accident into Gervais Street, yuppified old brick warehouses, abandoned train stations. The Blue Marlin restaurant shares with other establishments the Southern "Air Line" railroad station, originally built in 1904, authentic artifact from the old New South. Across the street is another restored terminal, long arched platform, now a restaurant called the Longhorn. Tex Mex touches Low Countries. Higher up, the Mellow Mushroom, at the periphery pawn shops and used tire stores eye these fires hungrily. Purists may pout, but what is there not to celebrate when human life flows back into abandonment in the Age of Katrina? By contrast, further west one finds the Riverbank Zoo and Botanical Garden, where the dark Saluda River marshily curves. To reach it one must also curve, a road playing tag with high-tension power lines, and penetrate a gated community named Saluda Mill. The power line skeletons have Saluda Mill covered. Right below them, its decorative central garden, a hypertensive lawn draped around imported primitive sandstone boulders and spring flowers on botox. With powerline skeletons, who needs gnomes? And the moral of it all is that the powerlines empower both the Blue Marlin and Saluda Mill. We they are.

Feast Day of St. Francis of Assisi, Patron Saint of Ecology

October 5,
Tybee Island, GA   **SHORE**

It is <u>hot</u>. Trinkets melt in tourists' hands. For poets, such oceanic shores have oft evoked time, pre- or post-lapsarian. These October surf kayakers clearly are unconcerned with time. They are paddling in the Now, cultivating their silhouettes. The beach is alive with the scent of barbecue. Artifacts of anxiety overlook Tybee Island's beach: historic black lighthouse (now tourist-topped), impenetrable Spanish American war

Sinking Creek Journal

barracks, now turned to other uses (one is a Shriners' clubhouse). Ancient brassy cannons welded to the earth. On the sand, deck-chair man tosses baby in air. Is this Mortality? Beyond the inleted planes of reeds towers a great angular structure. Nuclear power plant? No, slowly it moves. Tugboat guides it. Largest barge in the world, thousands of containers, containers of many colors. What do they contain? Perhaps it is a festal coffin ship, laden with the Earth's honored dead. Now that's a postlapsarian idea!

> "No matter how quiet the day, or how still the spruces baked in the summer sun, a slow, cool, sleepy sound hung over the island everywhere, a sound, it seemed, not so much of water as of air."
> Ruth Moore, **Speak to the Winds** (1956)

October 6   **AUTUMNAL PERSON**

Last night's slashing thunderstorm left a deeper—and chillier—sense of Autumn on Sinking Creek. It tore down the leaves of anticipation. Their definitive fall is already upon us. No mellow fruitfulness today, no swallows twittering in the skies. Oak leaves shower down, but slowly, some creating complex descent arcs of great ephemeral beauty. Against their trend are only new blue asters and late mushrooms—meaty milky caps, and a great cupped polypore, brown and white as from the potter's wheel. Today Ginger found, hidden under the sterile porcelainberry vine, a real pumpkin, unsuspected, of suspicious parentage, but real, emergent, a prince in disguise. But even the parasitic honeysuckle grasping the mailbox has turned yellow. What would they think on Tybee Island, only six hours south? Recognizable only would be the braided hibiscus with its one scarlet bud. As Whitman says, it is expressing itself, in October. What it is expressing is as yet unclear. Today, if he had lived, Father would be a hundred years old. He was a man for all seasons, master of none, but an Autumnal person. He wore autumnal clothes, and seemed to flourish wielding rakes in a flurry of leafpile creation. See him now, bending, tweed coat, to pry parsnips from the freezing loam.

> "Now in October I begin to feel myself akin, not with the katydid who dies or the woodchuck who hibernates, but with the squirrels

and the mice and the foxes, who stay awake."
Joseph Wood Krutch, **The Twelve Seasons**, 1949

October 7   PUFFBALL

Beside what is named the Nameless Stream, a semi-abandoned woodland garden trail—caught up short by a varnished white globe, more than a foot in diameter. Looks as though it's just landed from space, probably phoning home. Its cuticle glistens, antique white enamel. Last unripe member of a pack: a dozen ugly, crumpled, greenish-brown comrades surround it. This is ripe, not rot: only thus can they release their myriad spores. This is the giant puffball, *calvatia gigantea*. It is nice so many now flourish in fungal duff beside a purling stream. Nice to learn that it is a "choice edible," though probably not everyone's choice. Certainly, as suggested earlier, choice for youth to kick and stomp, watching the spores fly out. In the 1950's, the old days of wooded neighborhoods and unbuilt fields, they'd be brought to school to perform at recess.

" . . .*the smooth round swelling of the fungus made Liffey
think of a belly swollen by pregnancy* . . ."
Fay Weldon, **Puffball** (1980)

October 8   MUSHROOMS

A chilly morning in the woods. The first level of leaf-fall seems to have materialized in just 48 hours. A month from now, this path in a yellow wood will be almost invisible. Among the new leaf cover, great scatterings of acorns and fruits of the various nut tree species on the slope—post oak, pignut, shagbark hickory, butternut . . .

This harvest means good mast, happy black bears, contented hibernation (depending on temperature of course), fewer overturned trashcans and trashed bird feeders. There are also two new mushroom species, a reddish furl-capped one which looks like the ominously-named *delicious lacterius*, and a brilliant purple one of the clytocebe species, some of which are edible (like the *clytocebe nuda*, the "blewit"), and some deadly poison. Purple mushrooms seem to have great cultural resonance, providing the

Sinking Creek Journal

name of a band and of a problem in logic. We pass a tree stump salted with corn and fallen tree trunks that two days ago were aslant, propped by their fellows. Now, on the ground, they are, like the eroded puffballs, ripe, to fulfill their ultimate destiny, earth's decay and regeneration.

1981—*President Reagan lifts ban on commercial reprocessing of nuclear fuel*

October 9   **TROUT**

Hot afternoon, maples in flames. Absences are notable. Cool nights and warm days, the insects who would honor this warmth dead or in hiding, save a few compact yellow jackets. No flies in the wine. No tickling and welts on bare ankles. A single span survives the orb-weaver's complexity. A search for the undomesticated animate: pool in Sinking Creek under the sewer pipe. August of last year, pool drying, troutsaver came just too late, left with a freshly air-suffocated twelve-incher. It flows now, the only stream within our city limits unpolluted enough to support trout. Now another footlong one scoots beneath the concrete. Fingerlings scurry freshly. Two miles east, this same creek is lined with warnings against physical contact with its chemical self. We should be grateful for small trout. Water waders gang above them, their black shadows on the surface recall heavy galoshes on the dark father's feet.

1983—*President Reagan's controversial Secretary of the Interior, James Watt, resigns*

October 10   **OVERWINTERING**

Time to overwinter plants. Two days from now, night temperature will reach 32. The lipstick plant (blooms red and brushlike) which should have died five years ago moves in downstairs beside the bay tree, as does the lemongrass, rich with long thin spears the border collie Faye loves to munch. Beautiful orange calendula growing with it about to bloom. Upstairs, under east window, drusina spikes, braided hibiscus, the two New Guinea impatiens (this is an experiment) and three trays of elephant ears without their ears, tuskless. At the last minute the shamrock, squeezed below growlights. Today's warmth could have generated complacency, but, anthropomorphism: "My plants are safe" = "I am safe." Sip cabernet and the red-eyed dogwood berries glare down.

1963—Nuclear Test Ban Treaty takes effect

October 11   **POSTED**

"Posted" is the fresh trail sign today, where the cleared trail section commences, near the Bastian farmstead. Ratcheting sound uphill—is it being subdivided? It's hard to justify across-the-board criticism of new construction on old sites. All these Appalachian wooded hillsides have been logged, then farmed, second-grown, logged again, farmed again, third-grown . . .therefore the species diversity of trees, mix of conifers and hardwoods, hulking extinct chestnut stumps. But what does "posted" mean? Whatever the meaning, what physical space is "posted?" The space in front of the sign's observer? The encompassing space around the sign? What are its boundaries? If "posted" conditions access to a space, what are the conditions? What actually is posted? The earth itself? The foliage? Can deer and woodchucks be posted? It is all very confusing. Orlando says there are no clocks in the forest.

1939—Choking smog in St. Louis

October 12   **FINAL CUT**

Day of the final cut. Kenneth T. Jackson says the "lawn" evolved in the U.S. as a suburban requisite during 1840-1860; an "idealized view of the outdoors" gained dominance, "as humankind was removed from the real troubles of nature." The first push lawnmowers were invented in the 1860's. John Sumner patented the first self-powered [steam] lawnmower in 1893. The British aristocracy invented the scalp-trimmed lawn. The Sinking Creek neighbors must claim aristocratic status—they close-crop twice a week. Every suburban U.S. kid's father was or is a lawn fetishist. The sociology and psychology of the (usually) male and his lawn can be richly explored. Lawn and Order is the watchword. Our lawn, unlike the neighbors', is never pure. It is fertilized twice a year. Chemlawn and Mr. Green Thumb are banned. One year, mowing went electric, but our lawns are too eccentric: the electric machine exploded in rage. A compromise with pollution is the gas push mower. This day of the final cut wind lashes, clouds tear, there are sudden, brilliant, short-lived sun showers. Leif the border collie drops his tennis ball over and over by the mower, to force a throw. This is part of the job. The cucumber tree is about to release all its wide, flat leaves, but there aren't too many yet, so they are ground, crunched, mulched. Gnawed bones jostle and dull the blades. Dramatic drooping poisonous pokeberry says "don't mow under me." The youth used the time mowing Father's lawn to memorize all the kings of France. Now songs just repeat themselves autistically: "God didn't make little green apples . . ." Well then who did?

1976 — *Toxic Substances Control Act passed*

October 13   **BLACK AND WHITE**

A day too late to save basil planned to be clipped, bagged, hung indoors. Now every leaf hangs batwing black. Black too are the gourd and melon leaves, the fallen ironweed stems. White: three white-tailed deer fleeing, border collie tail tips plunging behind, surviving cosmos, bellyfur of freshly-killed roadside possum. Was that a white cabbage butterfly aloft still, or just a leaf falling oblique to the sun? Massive clump of dog fennel, hairy fountain ten feet high oblivious of this blackness. In fact, most leaves are still attached, green and unfallen. The death of the domesticated looms taller than the enduring light unblown.

"Autumn's clear cool days and crisp mornings, with Orion, the mighty hunter, high in the early southern sky, rekindle memories of barefoot days when we brought home the cows, shuffling our feet for a few moments in the warmth where the gentle creatures had lain." David Kline, **Great Possessions** (2001)

Fred Waage

October 14   **DUMP**

    Over-trimmed lawns frost white, while a quarter mile uphill, like snowfall, it aestheticizes the Burton Family Burial Plot for Inanimate Objects, a.k.a. the "dump." This trunk-pierced dump, where four trails meet, looks as it did a quarter-century ago—but, like life, closely observed it is ever-changing. Regions of tin cans, dead appliances, sink down, new ones rise. In a deeper region, sinkhole, moss-rimmed boulders, a whole colony of mattresses. Shattered sofa beds, even here sittable once, now rotted apart. The collies drink rainwater from an empty vacuum cleaner canister. Faye tiptoes carefully, sniffing for small rodents in this their Gothic palace. One upturned red water cooler has displayed the legend "Cold Melons" since time began. Bullet-plinked pails and paint cans cap windfall snags; often of a weekend revolver cracks, shotgun booms from up here fill the air: the highway patrolman is practicing. The dump must have been a collective enterprise since the first habitation. A garbologist might well find Civil-War era shattered pottery in its depths. No doubt it predates the forest that currently surrounds it.

> "The edge of the cancer
>   Swells against the hill—we feel
>   a foul breeze—
> And it sinks back down.
> The deer winter here
> A chainsaw growls in the gorge . . ."
>   Gary Snider, "Front Lines"

October 15   **COOL MENACE**

    Mid-month. Last night the collies were abark for hours at the forest edge. Raccoons? Bears? Today, clarity, light cirrus overhead, beauty and unrelenting cool menace in the air. Enough leaves have fallen for their oaky, healthy odor of decay to rise. Low sun makes light and dark patterns of surviving leaves on the pin oak's massive trunk. Plank bridge spanning springfed streamlet finally crashed underfoot. The neighbor's weimaraner splashes across Sinking Creek and inside his anguished cries lunges at the collies. One more unfrozen green tomato reveals itself. Almost all the butterfly bush's fragrant blooms are gone, along with their butterflies. Silence, save for the distant evening bark.

1966—National Wildlife Refuge System Administration Act passed

October 16   **RAIN BEGINS**

    Heavy rain drifting up from the southwest. You can smell it in the cold misty morning air. Clinchfield Railroad's bull-bellow whistle a mile away, coal car clatter audible all through the woods, as usual before a rain. Our contractor Paul visits. The melanoma on his cheek has returned, or is it only a cyst? He looks like he's wearing a twisted Happy Face. "I'm not afraid of Death," he says. The vultures have come back in force; they lift heavily *en masse* from the sycamores near the spring, or loom like black fruit, bending curious yet bored heads. A kingfisher chatters. The rain begins.

*1809—President Jefferson's Dunbar/Hunter Expedition
leaves to explore the lower Louisiana Purchase*

October 17   **TRAIL**

    Massive gusts, rainlashed breakers, crash white pine line in early morning darkness. Tossed leaves plack the face. Lighter, the ground is recovered with gold among the green. Wind, vulturian, gleans down dead twigs, small branches. Later we retrace the half-built trail along the Nameless Stream. All summer herbicide, otherwise rarely used, obliterated its poison ivy. Now the trail is paved slickly with sycamore and poplar leaves, it is hard to distinguish the poison ivy survivors from all the other saplets, but . . . aha—there are some still; footwash will be needed. The rock escarpments on the stream's north side shield the southside trees, so their north-facing bark is thickly mossed. Cross over plank bridge, shuffling through every color in the Brown God's paintbox, storm-felled rootmass makes cavern, menacingly inscrutable. Cross back again and come upon the Distinguished Puffball. No longer white, it is parchment yellow and, dead-center on it, an orange maple leaf, a perfect star.

Fred Waage

As every season has its own personality, so every trail has its own cadence." Paul Brooks, **Roadless Area** *(1942)*

October 18,
Port Republic, VA **POLLUTIONS**

 A countryside shattered by comfort: Al Gore Place, Rottweiler Hill, Pinball Lane, Purple Horse Road—a purple horse head rotating over a convenience store. What does it all mean? American chaos. Hot as summer. Kine graze happy pastures. Blue Ridge blueless, each tree a different degree turned, lucidly outlined. Respite from comfort: gravel road, horse and goats blackened in westering sun. Port Republic boat landing, where the North and South Rivers converge to form the South Branch of the Shenandoah. Stony Reach, complex current backflow, light glitter; the North Fork hot and silver, still, a few minnows. Heat on the withered sedge across, where no birds sing, grumble of rapids beneath the bridge, grumble of tractors, school buses on it. Sycamore leaves as edgy starfish underwater. Every tree is POSTED. Sagging wooden board full of warnings: don't eat any fish except stocked trout, all others may contain mercury, 80% of all smallmouth bass died in last two years: fungal infections . . .Up a few hills, the shattering begins again and every razed field is The Future Home Of——

1972—Clean Water Act signed

October 19, Yellow
Creek State Park, PA **LIVING SHORE**

 Roller coastering the ridges of Northern Appalachia, snaggly oaks in brown wheatfields—have they lost their leaves already? The altitude tells here. Abrupt hillsides are all yellow now. Ah, the Pennsylvania of Memory, truck-laden overcanopied roadways lined with rustic taverns. A respite, on a dock at Yellow Creek State Park. Morning's enveloping heavy mist has lifted, sun hot on the back, speckled clouds in water and sky, the shoreline ranks of hardwoods mistily aglow, organic pungency of a

Sinking Creek Journal

living shore, beds of browned cattails and thistles, where bobolinks bustle and gurgle, white-crowned sparrows cheep, red-winged blackbirds flash fire. Beach Capacity: 7,500—but concessions, lifeguard chairs, all happily abandoned now, all angularity and precision diminished. Solitary leaf fall acrobats into the gentling riffles. The Change so reluctant to change. Nor have the monarchs fled this place. Not yet.

> "The fall foliage—burgundy, scarlet, crimson, and saffron—lay reflected on the water as in a mirror. Tawny grass on the shoreline shimmered in the slanting sun. Spires of green spruces lanced the brilliant sky. . . . Back in the forest, a chipmunk went thunk-thunk-thunk. It was the only sound on this tremulous, golden, splendid day." Anne LaBastille, **Beyond Black Bear Lake** (1987)

October 20,
Indiana, PA   E<small>D</small>

Jim Cahalan gives an Edward Abbey tour today—Abbey's brother's house, his mother's church, his parents' grave. Tells many Abbey stories (driving the windy glorious leaf-strewn forest roads of Indiana County)—like his first hometown of Home, a hamlet named because its postmaster always took the mail *home* to sort it. Jim says Abbey's bioregional home was Crooked Creek, whose valley holds the ruins of many mining settlements. As a child, he moved with his family from home to home but always in shouting distance of Crooked Creek. The Jimmy Stewart museum, the statue of James Maitland Stewart before the Indiana County courthouse. Jimmy was always coming "home" to adulation, but one would think his real home was on the cover of *Life* magazine. Abbey, like his creek, wandered ever, but he knew his home was here. You can stand on the graveyard hill overlooking it, the ground between the stones all yellowed by pine needles, see through the pines the clean white shape of his mother's church, which he repudiated ("I'm not an atheist, I'm an eartheist"), and the swollen capping waters of his homestream forever flowing.

1991—California's worst forest fire, Oakland hills, kills 23 (to Oct. 24)

Fred Waage

October 21   **Nuts**

Wordsworth's great poem, "Nutting" recalls the "merciless ravage" of a mossy woodland "bower," leaving it "deformed, sullied," and "mutilated." Tobias Wolff in *This Boy's Life* describes a purgatorial assignment: cracking and demeating endless baskets of hickory nuts. Nutting may have passed on as a boyhood ritual, resulting sometimes in suffering—at least in suburban realms. Back then the boy and Father would take brown paper bags to the schoolyard where hickories grew tall, and, not ravaging, would gather them newly fallen in their coats. Father would pare them off and crack the nuts in his vise. Here, by late October, almost all this harvest has fallen into the paws of those truly in need of them, or their husks are rotting in the first stage of their decay toward spring germination, bombs of DNA and mass energy camouflaged from shallow human eyes but ready to explode with life . . . Still, the sweet pignut hickory's slightly ovate fruit lies smooth, sectioned open, the black walnuts, husks truly black, ribbed like brains, some intricately bored, the chinquapin spiny husk (tread softly), cracked open vulvularly, shell peeping out shiny as a mantelpiece . . .

1970—Dr. Norman Borlaug wins Nobel Peace Prize for innovating high-yield grain development in poor countries

October 22   **Shade**

Wet, dark, windswept day. Ginger has planted her spring pansies, they say we'll freeze tonight. Rainslick leaves are the woodland flooring. Still, autumnally speaking, we are ten days behind Northern Appalachia. Browsing among the understory saplings—how few will every find enough light to reach young adulthood—their very own parents overshadow them. Some may never even begin, like this furry green sycamore seedball, still attached to the twig it sprang from. Only some evergreens, attuned to shade, flourish under here—the three streamside rhododendrons, the hollies, the fat hemlocks with branches that drape down like tents, the perky dwarf junipers, waist-high cones of thorny needles. And of course maidenhair ferns, club moss, staghorn ferns, in the moist hollow we call the Fern Bar.

Sinking Creek Journal

1951—Nature Conservancy formed

October 23   **TREEKILL**

    Snow is suggested for tonight. Sure! Right! Driving the "Purple Heart Trail" near newest Wal-Mart's white desert roof, the wreckage where a corner of groomed green used to face three others of blacktop. When three have gone the fourth can never be far behind. There was agitation in our town, since four ancient beech trees grew on this vendible corner, trees arguably old as the first settler's cabin, which is historically marked across the freeway, between Food City and the animal shelter. Now the corner is chill churned dead weedcapped mounds of rubble. Its new owner did a stealth cut in the night. Now it is in a tangle of litigation as ugly and sterile as the land itself, though signage proudly announces Coming Soon: Millenium Towers. Millenium Towers—that's what it's all about.

"Ever since the cedars of Lebanon started going down to the sea in ships, we have failed to remember that photosynthesis makes it possible for creatures like us to breathe. The forest and forest soil are the essential elements of the Earth's thin, dynamic, beautiful skin." David Brower, **Let the Mountains Talk, Let the Rivers Run** *(1995)*

October 24   **MONARCH DEATH**

    So like a leaf in color and shape, the dead Monarch lies, wings spread, thorax twisted, in the dead center of the trail. How has it come to be here in high woods, the morning after frost? Did it wait too long to begin its epic trek South? Monarchs do not taste good, predators are aversive. This one's nutty orange wings are unshredded, immaculate. Was it suddenly frozen in high mid-flight, wheeling into this narrow crevasse a dead parachute? Earlier this summer, it was almost this same spot where a torn, struggling luna moth had to be mercy-stomped. This is different, a pure fatality. Let it join with its siblings the leaves as time melts them all into earth.

Fred Waage

"Winter is coming. I heard it last night. A moaning north wind
that ebbed and flowed like the sound of surf and ocean waves."
Bernd Heinrich, **A Year in the Maine Woods** (1994)

October 25   **ROOMS**

Rooms wherein you have imperceptibly aged, windowless rooms, the unperceived Autumn days curving one by one, no movement save dust, the invisible dust mites living their own swift cycles of life, the dead skin cells falling like leaves, rooms of necessary evasion, mementoes—the art of children, trophies of youth, adult souvenirs—denying and asserting permanence; and then the insufferable repetitive breathing, pulse of human chemistry in waves through walls conjoining the cold October wind . . .

"We can experience any place because we've all received, as part of
the structure of our attention, a mechanism that drinks in whatever
it can from our surroundings. This underlying awareness—I call it
simultaneous perception—seems to operate continuously . . . even
when our concentration seems altogether engrossed in something
else entirely." Tony Hiss, **The Experience of Place** (1990)

October 26   **EYES OF SUMMER PAST**

Very chill and grey, cloud *couvercle*, the only survivors from festal horticulture two calendula blossoms—one piercing yellow, one piercing orange, like the eyes of summer past bemused by the umber present. Such imaginary consciousness might wonder what transformation the hivernal turn of year will bring. See the two blossoms as spies sent across the equinoctial boundary to report the condition of a new land—no grapes here—blackened ironweed shafts, collapsed canna lily leaves. Surely, being natives to the kingdom of plants, they will see signs of the new land's own impermanence, the tight green buds at stembase patient, waiting through the months to come.

"And they told him [Moses] and said, We came unto the land
whither thou sentest us, and surely it floweth with milk and
honey; and this is the fruit of it." **Numbers** 13.27

October 27   **BIG WIND**

    Leaves piled like refugees on the deck, and blown pindrops glint every surface. Slow but steady cold rain all day, and with it the heaviest leaf-fall so far. Like proverbial snowflakes, each leaf has its individual curvaceous vertical trajectory, yet they become an unmingled collective at the end. Large sycamore leaves cloak like masks, the spoiled indoor plants placed outside to gather their last natural rich soaking of the year. Then, as the rain fails, wind strengthens, tearing leaves and needles horizontally eastward. Framed by comfort, the human can observe beauty in the misty muted colors, depthless backdrop, a painted cloth to all this violence, and the equally untouched methodical nuthatch bugging up and bugging down mossy pinoak trunk.

> "Where were the greenhouses going,
> Lunging into the lashing
> Wind driving water
> So far down the river
> All the faucets stopped?"
>   Theodore Roethke, "Big Wind"

October 28   **DAYLIGHT**

    Tonight those who observe it fall back from daylight savings time. Next year in the U.S. we will fall back later and spring forward earlier, in a great stroke against Global Warming. Like most eighteenth-century ideas, Daylight Savings Time was first proposed by Ben Franklin, but first legislated in the UK in 1916 to a storm of outrage and confusion. Fortunately, as with DST, there are no time zones in nature; quantitative time is a technological invention. In the U.S. it was invented for their convenience by railroads in the 1880's. DST in various forms was stolen for the convenience of U.S. warmakers. Only in the Uniform Time Act of 1966 was it defined nationally to run from the last Sunday in April to the last Sunday in October. Since then its *termini* have become as deeply rooted cultural rituals as the Super Bowl, and like most such rituals have validated themselves by taking on artificially the lineaments of nature.

Fred Waage

*1965—St. Louis Gateway Arch, symbol of
westward expansion, completed*

October 29   **GIDDY LUCIDITY**

In keeping with the season, we contacted the Ghosts of Collies Past on the Ouija board. Cobweb told Leif to take care of Faye and "stay golden." The Big Wind, still slightly gusting, has defoliated all; streams are blue and the forest floor is all gold, but we know it will not stay. Morning sun, clear sky create a giddy lucidity, patterns aslant trunks, reveals hidden windfalls, reached to touch the foreshadowed ground ivy and staghorn fern. Leaf-shrouded waste patches unveiled show what ravages the southern pine bark beetles have wrought upon our minority conifers. Slant of light lends separate tones to each trunk. Many living trunks, having shed after years the dead weight of neighbors, still gratuitously bow. Most evocative are newly-revealed old fence posts, vinously standing, raddled with rot. Rusty barbed wire twists around them. These are the tomb-makers of ownership and containment. You can imagine the sectioned, pastured, corn-grown, wavy slopes before abandonment and second coming of trees.

"I live on an island of sanity: the island of this place . . . I no longer ask why. The small animals, the birds go about their ancient and patterned ways. They do no enlarge their territories or change their patterns in order that they may kill and die more quickly . . . They do not know what we are doing. They do not know what we have done." Josephine Johnson, **The Inland Island** (1969)

October 30   **MOMENTARY WARMTH**

Heat has spiked up this afternoon. The sky is clear and early-lowering sun again glares horizontally between pine trunks. Gnats in the wine, true sign of warming. The spike falls all too soon, though, and creatures unresistant to cold are frozen in their illusion. Down beside Sinking Creek, water flows clear and fast, oblivious clusters of snails on every underwater

Sinking Creek Journal

rock. Springs and seepages enhance the flow here, where the stream bends, and under stone near one a dusky salamander s-curves. Touched, it scarcely moves. Is the moving water enough to keep it living, semi-hibernal, through the months to come? Tennis ball picked up to throw for Leif—an ichneumon fly is on top of it, wobbling like a drunkard. Unladed on the table, it staggers, tentative, seeming stunned and too cold to take wing. It is a spot of rich amber, melting into the Japanese cherry leaves.

1948—*Donora smog disaster begins*

October 31   **HEADLESS ANGELS**

Oak Hill Cemetery, the first one in our town, now devandalized, mowed, its green defies the season. Once it was at the edge of town; now, a large rectangle, surrounded by low income housing, warehousing; between stone columns one can read "Kelly Foods." Crows are the caretakers here, caw from tree to tree, congregate on the one leafless one. Tall oaks, elms, and spruces scatter the cemetery thinly. At its highest point, an immense bigleaf magnolia has pushed stones aside, scarlet fruit on its long cones. The dead cluster by families here: Ranges, Cloyds, Stonecyphers. Headless angels brood, eroded lambs curl up, imitating the season a topless, limbless cement treetrunk proclaims a life cut short. This fresh expanse speaks, now, of endurance and renewal. Death may hold terrors, but the dead seem welcoming. Just by the gate there is a fresh monument, must have cost a bundle, carven and tinted middle landscape in autumn, deer below yellow trees: a sort of metamonument. Fisher Mickey/Sherry—no dates. They must be still alive, waiting to decay beneath the autumn scene: "I have lived my life/Now go live yours."

> "And we were conscious of the beautiful, nearly finished little cedar building at the edge of the firelight, this 'new organization' of our world and life, each member of our family, in a complex, independently proprietary way, as if it were a poem we were all writing together." Charles Gaines, **A Family Place** (1994)

November 1   **GRASSHOPPER**

Warm again, clouds darkening down the valley, cold front moving in. Still on the brick housewall, a red-legged grasshopper, so close a slight headbump would crush it. What heat there is the bricks absorb and slowly disgorge as the air cools. So in this still moment of time, and energy oasis, the still grasshopper is a drinking buddy. Eyeballed, it shows neither recognition nor fear. Red lower legs match the brick, brown thorax is trim. This is a well-groomed grasshopper. An eastward migrant, it appears to bear no personal guilt for its species' soybean ravishments. It has its feet on the brick, it knows where it is, it has its own static agenda. As everything darkens, even the leafgold fades, we go in and soon hear rain drumming. In next morning's chill the grasshopper is still there, its position only slightly altered. Maybe it will be a feature of the house forever, Bartleby of grasshoppers.

*1990—U.S. signs London Dumping Convention to
end all dumping at sea of industrial waste*

November 2   **WILD NESTS**

Bared branches now reveal the homes of avian neighbors, abandoned but not inchoate. Just along the trail, at least seventeen squirrel or crow nests. Both are messy (to human eyes) builders. Higher on the mountain, their stick and leaf clumps stand out more clearly, since the trees have less remaining foliage. Most nests are in high crooks, or balanced on high hardwood branch tangles. A whole generation has been raised on these steppes, unbeknownst to humans doing their own cycles. The childhood house was constructed in an old orchard. In fall 1950's children would scurry up and down the apple trees, gathering the aesthetically hollowed nests of songbirds, especially robins, once even a Baltimore oriole's hammock. This cold wet woods is less tamed, less shaped in the human image than that one. Though their builders are partly our dependents, and dwell for sustenance near our dwellings, these wild nests still seem to bristle somewhat out of the anthropocentric blanket in which we nestle.

1992—President Bush signs bill prohibiting drift net fishing

Sinking Creek Journal

November 3   **LAKEFRONT**

TVA lakefront, narrows, green-mown terrace, dandelion surprise. Midafternoon, empty boatramp to slimy stonefill, the lake is drawn down ten feet or more for winter, its usual marge on the rockface across is a black line like a bathtub ring. On this side, wire mesh holds in a crushed shale mini-dike where a metal detector trolls. On the water is a trolling red motorboat. On the other side, hidden behind the gold, a trolling leafblower. Solitary mechanicals. Killdeer alight, troll the sandy mudflats. The big highway crosses where the lake broadens. "Lakeside Condominiums" rise where once youth dangerously rock-plunged. Here, lights on, the work-crew convict bus, idling. Don't ask why. Caught in the net.

"*In the United States—as elsewhere—we have impounded rivers, let them fill with silt, and sickened them with wastes beyond accounting. We still have within our technologies the means of helping rivers to regain their health . . .*" William H. Amos, **The Infinite River** (1970)

November 4   **MULCH**

Real freeze last night—crystals rime every leaf, and even the holdouts like calendula have withered out the fight. Flurries at the thistle bags. Collies love the brittle, cracking air. Faye always runs ahead, poised, midtrail, waiting white chest triangle, sharp black eyes, pink tongue. But now it is time to put the gardens to bed. Goldfinches no longer peck the dead sedum stalks. The mulch man's trailer is surrounded: pyramidal black mulch, brown mulch, red mulch, super red mulch. He's got playground mulch, flower bed mulch and moo poo, which sounds like a Chinese dish but makes sense if you think a second. Run your hands through them (except the last), feel the texture, imagine how each one would lie three inches thick over you, you a bound living root or bulb, a shape of life waiting.

"*Even in the driest summers, harvesters can strip only an inch or two from the surface of a bog per year. The peat that requires months*

to gather up, however, may have taken more than a century to lay down. In all but glacial time, peat is a nonrenewable commodity." Roger B. Swain, **Saving Graces** (1991)

November 5   **IN THE WAY**

We are in the way. Bluejay bangs the picture window, flutters drunkenly to the pinoak, shaking its head. Why do these collisions increase in Autumn? Is it the slant of light? Half a dozen recently. Commonly no fatalities, no telltale feather-smears from cat predation. Knocked cold, they come around, fly off. It has been suggested to stick post-it notes on the glass, to signal solidity. Is it hypocritical for the environmentalist to resist this idea? Considering how overwhelming human construction is destroying habitat . . . should we return to caves? Consider the deer. In this chunk of forest-facing suburbia, wild strips, corridors between human habitats are their caravanserai and roadways. A deer's positive photograph of the Sinking Creek valley would be a negative. This afternoon three chorusing collies freeze a doe midway its corridor across the creek, a solitary doe poised mid-passage. Finally collies are distracted, she leaps, swift absolute grace, across the back yard, up the hillside. We are in the way.

"The grazing herd . . .shows a state comparable with the City of the **Laws** *of Plato: communality and disciplined orderliness which need but little discipline. Environmental conditions being equal, territories are bounded by choice and not by jealousy."*
F. Fraser Darling, **A Herd of Red Deer** (1937)

November 6   **LATE MIGRANTS**

This is the season, says our local expert, when the last wave of migrants from the North passes through, or, in many cases, comes to stay for the winter. This is their Caribbean. Right on cue, in early twilight, white-crowned sparrows are hopping under the feeders and pecking at the browned ecinacea heads. Another, slate-colored junco, border collie of birds—sleek black hood, grey side, white front, when it jerks about in flight, hidden white tailfeathers flash. It dances in the dogwoods to a different drummer than do the *habitués*—chickadees, titmice, cardinals—with a species-specific body (or birdy) language, exotic resonance. Stepping back in acquaintance, one realizes how much recognition, especially among bare branches, depends on familiarity of rhythm: the hop, the launch into flight, the flight pattern. Even dull winter-plumaged, the goldfinch flies in scoops and dips, molding its identity in motion.

"Goldfinches in dull winter plumage were flying between trees in swooping flight, singing as they do in summertime on each dip. Cardinals, chickadees and nuthatches were jostling one another at the feeder. On the ground . . . small, trim, neat gray-and-white [juncos] were scratching for weed and grass seeds so earnestly that they did not even fly up as I walked among them."
Sue Hubbell, **A Country Year** (1983)*

November 7   SECOND IN TIME

   High on this shoulder of Buffalo Mountain, the trees are brown, but the encroached pastures are still green; black horses graze dramatically. Blue tears through the cloud cover. Vines, green still, enlace hay bales. Here one feels on a baby Wyoming, enskyed prairie, air illusorily fresher. Forget the factories, the suicidal old railroad underpass, the double-wide clutter, face away from the misplaced ranch houses still displaying Halloween ornaments, look over the Southwestward wooden fences and feel for a moment transported in that direction, beyond Appalachia. But Appalachia looms forever. Head uphill, pass an incongruous stone mansion resembling the headquarters of a Nazi cult, and the rhododendron-rimmed stream slit enfolds you, you realize you've but stood a second in space-time, inside an isolated irregular pause of a persistent heartbeat.

1973—President Nixon calls for national energy self-sufficiency by 1980

November 8   AUTUMN GREEN

   In November the woodland greens again, especially as today, a drenching rain past, the leaf cover almost gone, the minority conifers dominate, mainly spruce, widespread arms aspiring laterally to the sun. This is a boulder field forest: every rock, crag, every hardwood trunk, windfallen tangle, is green with mosses and lichens—ruffle and loop lichen from undulant topographies on beech and hickory, their lobules lapped out like tiny cresting waves. Thick-bunched anomodon mosses clump where trunks divide at the base, or on stones half-sunken in the duff. Leucobrum mosses form discrete landscapes, large or small, on the forest floor. The Fern Bar is the greenest space of all. Where a very occasional stream bed spreads into a mini-cove, seepage has enabled this diverse mixed-race moss colony. Running cedar undergrows all and shapes a verdant tableland amid the forest.

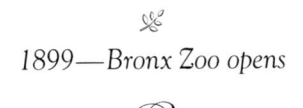

1899—Bronx Zoo opens

November 9   **SALAMANDERS**

Idly climbing a wet slope, collies barking far ahead. The Burton dump. Turn aside a leaf-drowned log, careful not to disturb the surviving golden trumpet mushroom colony clinging to it. Startled into immobility underneath, where fallen fragments of former plant life are happily, warmly rotting, is a young yonahlossee salamander. This salamander has a rich crimson back, black head, tail, and legs. The log is carefully replaced, but now, uptrail, almost every well-seated log seems to shelter one of these salamanders. Further uphill are found a dusky salamander, a two-lined salamander, but no more of those streaks of red. They create wonder at the secret life everywhere hidden from dull human eyesight in the Autumn forest.

1969—Native American occupation of Alcatraz begins

November 10   **AIRSHOW**

Indian summer. Warm light glistens. Miraculous moths veer. High school girls sunbathe. Hot white light off freight tracks and metal roofing of abandoned factories. Gunning 4 X 4's roar at 70 on 40 mph two-lanes. Exuberance before the front. Jet trails V-converge to the west, immerse their junction in slow-gathering white clouds. The trails' rigidity disperses haltingly while vultures loop organic form within and around them. At the right tilted angle the dropping sun metals their wingtops to match the trails. V for Victory? Vanity? Velveteen Violence? Vulture? Some predators cleanse the world of offal; some spread it through blue air.

1986—Emergency Wetlands Resources Act passes

November 11   **MILKWEED**

Almost no milkweed pods remain unsplit and unspilled, sparse below distinctive blackened ironweed flowerheads (the ironweed leaves, dog-eared, dangle). One stalk's pods, browned, are still hard. Another's cotton hangs down, the seeds are still clumped, entangled. The fluff feels moist. Will the next bout of gusts just fell them altogether? Can we assume the knowledge untangling and releasing them implies? This backlot bordering the Nameless Stream is to be kept a wild field. Saplings are regularly cut to inhibit reforestation. Is this tampering with progression justified? As a wild field, without leaf cover, it furnishes a feast bank for insects and birds, and unscheduled flourishment for every variety of native—and some non-native—wildflowers, from tall yellow mullein spikes, to low-clumped white maidens' bower, to the bridal pink bloom clusters of milkweed, milkweed so widely threatened by de-wilding that every plant preserved and seed wafted abroad is renewal for the endangered life forms so dependent on it, especially the monarch of all, the Monarch itself.

1867—Granger Movement founded by Oliver Kelley

November 12   **SPRING CLEARANCE**

A grey chill afternoon, out to clear the spring—not the pasture spring (how many readers assume wrongly that Frost's is a springtime poem?), but the spring that springs under a high-towered backyard tulip poplar, then flows streamlet-wise along lawn verge to bog garden pool, and so onward to join the much wider outflow from Sinking Creek spring itself, hence into the Nameless Stream, which, mingled waters, enhances the alpha creek. Collies now bark in amaze as from that creek rises—like a stunt pilot's liftoff—between towering sycamores, a great blue heron, its seven-foot wingspan with assured grace not grazing a single branch. The heron lives far downstream, probably where sunken Sinking Creek enters the broad Watauga River, but even in winter visits occasionally for shallow-water fishing, snails galore. Every heron rise is a surprise. While the collies reflect, frozen hands raise spadefulls of leaf-laden rich erosive soil out of the streamlet; old jewelweed stalks and pulpy fallen canna lily stems are clipped. Sacrosanct horsetails are spared, every watercress colony impeding the flow is lifted. The stream and pond life seems gone underground now, the only life disrupted that of brown fishing spiders that zone down to safe haven till this holocaust has passed.

> "I'm going out to clean the pasture spring;
> I'll only stop to rake the leaves away
> (And wait to watch the water clear, I may):
> I shan't be gone long.—You come too."
> Robert Frost, "The Pasture"

November 13   **NO DARKNESS**

Sounds carry far in this leafless chill. Collies clamor woodsward every few minutes, evening barks spread downstream like water molecules, become cyclical like water itself as downstream barks inspire upstream ones and then the ones right here again. To the human ear there's Nothing out there, to the canine, some stealthy Truth, a Presence—raccoon, deer—not annunciatory like bobcats, coyotes, bears, who've come down the mountain before. The bare skin feels condensing mist—if a living statue overnight, one would wake with frost on every hair. The city's light pollution also bounces off clouds and into eyes. However close wild presence may be, there's no true darkness here.

1958—United Nations Conference on the Law of the Sea (to Nov. 17)

November 14   **ORANGE**

High ridge, abandoned Bastian farmsite cleared, farther back only one lean-to still standing: corner posts, sagging roof, some sort of dyed burlap, folded, something in camouflage gear. The clearers had a hard time with the introduced, overgrown plants, particularly the sprawling, thorn-stemmed shrub, trifoliate orange (*poincirus trifoliata*), startling to meet first twenty years ago when this dooryard was not long abandoned. Left unkempt, it had climbed and encircled all the old trees. Fortunately three oranges were brought downhill, but now here their spiny skeletons, white in death, have been bulldozed into heaps. When flourishing, they bear perfectly circular, hard, bright orange fruit an inch in diameter, proclaiming alien status. One, twenty feet tall, seems to have intimidated even the dozers, at its base a green spinefield of new growth, and all around a litter of those hard orange balls.

"The November 209, 1966, photograph showed fully cleared fields to the west of the footpath to the cabin, and in the area where the cabin now stands. The surrounding, stonewall-enclosed field to the north of the cabin, the area that is now my sugar maple grove, looked like a cleared field except for a few scattered young pines. The old field to the west that is now my pine grove showed a gradation from scattered to continuous young pines." Bernd Heinrich, **The Trees in My Forest** (1997)

November 15　　　　　　　　**RAKING**

The rake raises up the bones of summer past. They roll between tines, left behind as freed grass breathes. The raker also breathes, returns, rescrapes again reluctant pine needles. Flower beds the raker leaves alone, knowing nature's own mulch will richly feed them. Except the raking, there's only weekday silence, no leaf blowers from Hell polluting every sense. The neighbors' lawns are already buzz-cut, leaf-blown to the roadside where an orange truck—itself like a leaf deformed by gigantism—will, belching exhaust, sanitarily dispose of them. The neighbors pretend to have no space for leaves. The primitive raker has brushy borders everywhere, lifts armloads over the skeletons of Christmas trees past, piles of fallen limbs. Returns. More bones. And here the skin, the tail, the feathers, of a chickadee. RIP

1806—Zebulon Pike sights Pike's Peak

Fred Waage

November 16   **LAUGHING BRANCHES**

    Big night wind—much bigger in the South from whence it came of course. Branches lash and clash. Morning reveals a twigfest, the neighbors' careful leaf piles respread. The long driveway is full of branches which love to catch themselves under cars and laugh at the asphalt. Sinking Creek valley is a sheltered spot—no tornadoes here. The sun falls swiftly, swiftly chill spreads. Wind rises, usually an erratic presence. The litter of its steady force last night shows only on the spaces the humans have cleared. Up in the woods it is embraced by and assimilated to the infinite variety of the organic. Got to stop the car and pull free that obnoxious branch to stop its laughter.

" . . . hide in the hills of the Hollow, lave in its waters, tan in its golds, bask in its flower-shine, and your baptisms will make you a new creature indeed. Or, choked in the sediments of society, so tired of the world, here will your hard doubts disappear, your carnal incrustations melt off, and your soul breathe deep and free in God's shoreless atmosphere of beauty and love." John Muir, "Twenty Hill Hollow" (1872)

November 16   **TINY SNOW**

    First snow today—but scarcely snow—tiny pinhead flakes, short and tingling rushes. Evanescent, nothing left behind except the scent of purity in the air, the surfaces of things densely lightened; pewter sky shades to white above treetops. A climacterical time, the duration, short or long, of this first snow, like that between when the child has pulled his sled to the top of the hill, turned it, flopped down, and when he kicks off. Once upon a time when real children had real sleds these moments occurred often, in preglobalwarming places where the drifts didn't melt from December to March. And here again, nonetheless, the rush of that first descent, in time, space, memory.

"In civilization we try to combat winter. We try to modify it so that we can continue to live the same sort of life that we live in summer. . . . Naturally

it doesn't work very well. You can neither remodel nor ignore a thing as big as winter." Louise Dickinson Rich, **We Took to the Woods** (1942)

November 17,
Shenandoah Valley, VA   **INTERSTATE**

On pastures green as spring, black angus lyrically prepare themselves to become Angus 'n Shrooms. Low sunset behind them bars trunks. Through their slats flash red, white, blue lights, like carrion flies they surround racked up trucks, shrieking cellphone cellophane girls. Overtaken, dead elms end-droop decaying multichimneyed brick mansions. We are on the high road to success, where there are no seasons. Petroleum leaks from tanks into Cedar Creek where Sheridan smashed the Rebels. All's Right with the World.

1969—First round of SALT talks begins in Helsinki

November 18,
Annapolis, MD   **ARTIFICE OF CELEBRATION**

All the shopkeepers, with one accord, this afternoon, are raising the Christmas greens, interminable strings of plastic pine needles and red bows, uniting commerce in a pre-Thanksgiving artifice of celebration. The shopkeepers' dogs, tied to parking meters, mingle with the humans in a wilderness of ladders. By contrast, the careless unseasoned Bay waters slap pilings in eternity. The Save the Chesapeake sailboat spreads its banner. In window boxes real roses and marigolds bloom still, in Christmas shops hang horseshoe crab ornaments. At wet chill dark, only boat light reflections betray the water—just above it polychromic ruggers hurl energy as though all seasons were one.

*"Despite its occasionally obnoxious manifestations, the celebration
of the local is a healthy impulse, a resistance to homogenization,
an attempt to define and center ourselves where we are, and
consequently to value and preserve our local landscapes."*
Deborah Tall, **From Where We Stand** (1993)*

November 19,
Mint Spring, VA   **ORDERED SPACE**

 A brick house set back on a sloping rise. Paired windows, dark blue shutters, between two cut stone chimneys. Slate roof, white doorway arch, gazebo in back. In this house 1800 triumphs over the trailers, double-wides, whitewashed wideporched tinroofs of 2000. Long after passing, this house remains. When the valley road spilled the Scotch-Irish south and over the mountains this house was sternly in this place and probably fronted an empire of cropland. It was a sentinel of future permanence to the transmontane peoplers, the Appalachian forest slayers. It suggested the propagation of ordered space. In this sense its classic symmetry is imperial, admonitory. The round grey clouds press down on its unseasonable green lawn.

"The present resonates with its full meaning only when the past is right behind it like the skeleton beneath the skin. Fortunately for me, the landscape I live in is irregular with the juttings of history. Daily, I am reminded of the need to work on this business of preservation." Peter Svenson, **Preservation** (1994)

November 20   **FEEDER BIRDS**

 Livid clouds above, *en masse*, and between each mass a blazing brevet of silver, even though here on earth the air is still. These are not silver linings. No sky opens beyond them. The feeder birds have exhausted their supply these three grey days, retreated to more natural plucking where the gaunt brush scrabbles. Now, alert to movement, the human consciousness personifies their beady eyes and chattering gossip. There are those who oppose feeders on the neoconservative grounds that they make the birds dependent on human dole. How ridiculously anthropocentric! Humans possess and have excused the power to destroy species through destroying habitat, but not through enhancing it.

*1969—USDA bans DDT in residential areas as first
step toward a total ban planned for 1971*

Sinking Creek Journal

November 21   **TRUE FREEZE**

25 degrees this morning. A true freeze has settled. Only the parsley survives. Skidding the white grass, slipping and scrambling up the mountain, almost prone, grasping at roots. The collies dance ahead. Why weren't humans given padded paws? All the ground leaves slick with frozen condensation, it's like skating uphill. Where the earth is bare, tiny intricate ice constructions crunch underfoot. The fern fronds and holly leaves have white rims. Twigs crack precise and sharp. Unit B deer hunting season for guns began November 18, but no members of the orange-vested tribe are yet in evidence. Return with a trophy of frozen hands and tail wags.

1964—Verazzano Narrows Bridge opens

November 22   **GREAT TREES**

Much of this college campus was once a great estate, its English landscaping has preserved trees and contours of terrain. Now on a grey cold morning the great trees which made it through the change reveal their magnificence, naked against the sky. Much has been done to afforest this campus; many lower native and non-native trees are scattered, now bare as the signs that name them. All the giant trees, though, are natives—from the 200-year-old white oak to the centenarian ironwood. Many of the great trees rise in spaces awkward relative to human construction, suggesting the constructors consciously preserved them. There is a certain consolatory irony in this survival: their individuation is the product of selective arboreal destruction. The campus's 75-year-old buckeye is cherished, while one in the woods next door is twice as old, twice as tall, and nameless. Unfortunately, it seems that far too often rarity breeds contempt, not preservation.

> *"These are not young trees starting out fresh against the elements. The oak and madrone have withstood the ravages of cold, heat, wind, fire, roads, and insects. And they are still here. This is a mark of ecological wisdom, the intelligence of survival, the simple act of living through it all."* Stephanie Kaza, **The Attentive Heart: Conversations with Trees** *(1996)*

November 23   **SOUND POLLUTION**

Sound, particularly in these leafless times, pollutes the echoing wood. It rises, an aural smog tectonic, from western road-creased valleys, or descends, burping veils, from the Medical Center's ER helicopters, rushing to raise the stricken out of their deep Appalachian coves. If this were the forest primeval, one would hear only paws and feet scuffling leaves, an occasional crowcall. Now, at the trail's height, there is still an indefinable bass continuo. Further down are recognizable motor accelerations, the ubiquitous leaf blowers, the unverbalizable diversity of machinery, gearing in and gearing out. There are those no doubt who can identify a machine by its call as surely as a birder can a bird. It would be strange to walk these woods with one who, cocking an ear, could say "ah, yes, a backhoe," or "clearly, a bobcat on rough terrain." It is difficult to characterize sound pollution nonjudgmentally, by air impact as distinct from source. How would one feel hearing the call of an endangered bird, if it sounded exactly like a backhoe?

> "At every halt he made it a game to discover what he could hear. Often, after he had turned off the engine, he heard nothing at all, even in a town. Sometimes there was the chirp of a bird or the faint humming of an insect; sometimes the wind made a little rustling. Once he heard with a sense of relief the muffled pounding of a far-off thunderstorm." George R. Stewart, **Earth Abides** (1949)

November 24   **PLANTING GARLIC**

Now is a time to plant garlic, *alium sativum*. The alium garden is overshadowed by a massive dog fennel waterfall, which must first be cut back. At this point the chives' browned flowerstems still survive, and one old limping sage. Higher, ghastly ancient crabapple's twisted shadow reaches towards it. Nonendemic garlic is victimized by every ill a bulb is subject to, most particularly moist rot. The best adapted to Appalachia is Polish white, which contradictorily blushes purple. Unfortunately it is not available. So anyway the autumn drift is cleared, to make sure the planting

Sinking Creek Journal

displaces no one underground. The papery Kroger cloves are separated delicately from their bulbs, a good layer of new topsoil is spread, and each clove goes in an inch, root end down, at four-inch intervals. A clear bright day, close to the soil, the intimate odor of dormancy. Now all we—cloves and humans—can do is wait, grow in our different ways when we can, guard against the early intemperate weeds.

"The earth is given as a common stock for man to labour and live on. If, for the encouragement of industry we allow it to be appropriated, we must take care that other employment be furnished to those excluded from the appropriation. If we do not the fundamental right to labour the earth returns to the unemployed." Thomas Jefferson, to James Madison, October 28, 1785

November 25   **GUNFIRE**

Mid-woods, pepsi can pistol sculpture, finally tumbled from its 2-month treetrunk perch, twisted and torn, the aluminum skin invested now with organic form like leaf blades. Midafternoon, small arms fire, repetitive, back up there. State trooper plinking cans in his dump again. 'Tis the season, we're the trigger on the rifle belt. The views now clear, abandoned camouflage blinds, slops, sinkholes—big nests left by dangerous predators. TEEN SCORES EIGHT-POINT BUCK ON FIRST KILL. COP SCORES EIGHT-FIGURE DEALER ON FIRST KILL. Right?

"The reports of the fire-arms became rapid, whole volleys rising from the plain, as flocks of more than ordinary numbers darted over the opening, covering the field with darkness, like an interposing cloud; and then the light smoke of a single piece would issue from among the leafless bushes on the mountain, as death was hurled on the retreat of the affrighted birds, who would rise from a volley, for many feet into the air, in a vain effort to escape the attacks of man." James Fenimore Cooper, **The Pioneeers** (1823)

November 26   **ROPE OF MEMORY**

About fifteen years ago Melissa, fresh from camp, roped trees where the trail is steepest, curves above a rock face, dubbed it Dead Man's Pass.

The rope rail holds now, as glove glides down it, boulder steps and slippery leaves; what to make of its presence and the absence of its maker? The house is small, but open house was kept, they lived in the immanence of nature, splashed the streams, dared copperheads, observed kestrels scoop up songbirds, witnessed the births of puppies, the burials of cats. Holding on this rope of memory now. They left with those gifts outdoor childhoods can bestow, such as this rope of consolation in remembrance of things past.

"Here in the Allegheny Mountains, in my third return to earth, I live on top of a hill, and I hope I can stay, though I miss the sounds of farming that abide in memory . . . The fields I can see in winter when the leaves fall are not mine, though why I should wish to own fields to look out upon is a vagary explainable only by the vistas of my childhood on that first farm." Virginia Bell Dabney, **Once there Was a Farm** (1990)

November 27   **DAMSITE**

Boone Dam on the Holston River—still, straight, warm noon; the flags flop. Bare trunks' shadows bar the hillside. Silver birds periodically gain altitude overhead. Lake drawn down, mudflats stretch out far beyond the curve of imported sand. There's a map of the Tennessee River Watershed, and a cutaway of its sequential dams. There's a self-laudatory text about the TVA: "Integrated, Balanced, Efficient." Boone Dam was constructed in 1952. It is 188 feet high. Old homes, traditional rurality, clip the territory, unlike the condominium-gutted farms along the highway to this place. Peer down, a power grid, shockingly large junglejim of energy, fills the gorge. Drive a bit, look back, the impenetrable wall somehow frightening. Static, blank, it seems in virtual motion downstream, threatening to cut off everything that flows.

1926—Restoration of Colonial Williamsburg begins

November 28   **RUNNER BEANS**

Picked the scarlet runner beans today. They sure are runners. This is the third or fourth generation, and although planting recommendations

Sinking Creek Journal

have not been followed, they've multiplied and propagated more with each replanting, climbing every grid that will give them purchase—decking, fencing, tree stumps. Their flower clusters scream at every pollinator, demanding service, and their tangle is abuzz all day. Now it's all brown, the dead leaves hang, the pods, curved even spiral, antic shapes and sizes, mottled black. The pods are so well camouflaged within the carcasses of parent plants, the harvester has to keep returning to what had seemed stripped before. The greatest pleasure, though, is the shelling, for the beans within unmildewed pods are spectacularly smooth, varnished, also mottled brown and black, but a shiny light-reflecting black, to display the transcendent craft of a Master/Mistress.

"I was determined to know beans." Henry David Thoreau, **Walden** (1845)

November 29 **WALKING THE LINE**

Between our property and one neighbor's stretches the white pine line. Imperceptibly, inevitably, over a quarter century the pines have reached a castellated height, their lower limbs pruned, died, so there are none to block the cross-boundary gaze. Since Branna is a collie who aggressively responds to alien sound and sight, who bears contempt for boundaries, she did once therefore evoke Animal Control by trespass. This resulted in a hundred feet of fencing, stapled to the pine trunks and draped with opaque green tarp. Sinking Creek valley's winds swoop downstream, periodically unanchoring the fence and kiting out the tarp. So today, when autumn has defoliated poison ivy, the line again is walked, imitating a famous spring stone ritual. Downed and leaning limbs, in-your-face brush scrabbles clothing, hands brush the telltale furry poison ivy vines. It is a windfall ballet but not, not, an argument for the saying of Robert Frost's neighbor. It is not custom but necessity, one argues, while the saucy wee bitch Faye mocks from the neighbor's forbidden side.

" . . .once the idea of a fence had planted itself in my mind, it grew and grew until I had convinced myself that it must surround the entire eighty acres . . . But I have no doubt . . . I was also driven, like the anoles on the rafters of the house and the singing, quarrelling birds in the surrounding *woods, by an instinctive need to stake out a territory and defend it against all comers."* Don Schueller, **A Handmade Wilderness** (1996)

November 30   **Pileated Woodpecker**

Mr. Ki, the Most Favored Cat of the House, enters, mud-cloaked, soaked to the skin, someone else's blood on his fur. The mud is rank and putrid, but there is no rank and putrid mud around this house, no disturbances in the bog garden. Run-in with raccoons? Coyote? There are no answers to these questions. Much is concealed. Later, the pileated woodpecker booms as we mount the trail. Despite bare branches, its hugeness is rarely seen in flight. Orally ahead when we go uphill, ahead when we go down. And then, sometimes, it is dramatically too close—clawed to the cucumber tree, squatting on a stump. Domestic or wild, the creatures feel no need to confess, to reveal. That is a specifically human failing.

"Last year a pileated woodpecker spent several weeks cutting big, oblong cavities in a ten-inch birch just over the hill from my house. He cut eight such holes, for some reason I never understood, and so weakened the tree that a windy rainstorm took down its whole top." Hal Borland, **Beyond Your Doorstep** (1962)

December 1   **Condo Site**

The front has slashed through like a sharp wet knife, leaving gusts, a clear sky, and silvered surfaces. An empty field that once grew corn slopes gently toward Sinking Creek. It has been mowed, but the grass is long, the blades glint. Amazingly, it remains unexcavated. Amazingly, because it was bought to become a condo community. But many years before, prepubescent and archaeological, Erick found between its cornstalks a treasury of Woodland Indian arrowheads, flint shards, spear points, resulting in its state registration as an archaeological site. Apparently the field's neighbors have used his artifacts successfully at least to stall the developers. As around this nation, those aeons dead preserve land for the living. Now the field stretches a quarter mile, to fluffed dead kudzu mats and a burnt house's foundations filled with trash—which will be the field's fate, if it becomes a built environment, sometime in the coming aeons.

Sinking Creek Journal

1958—International treaty designates Antarctica as a wildlife and scientific preserve

December 2   **SURROUNDED**

Our city's once surreptitious beltway encircles rural space, thus "urbanized" so the encircled rural space can be "filled in." Of course, these rural spaces are already full, highly developed as plant and animal residential areas. One such abandoned farmsite is already embattled: the "Med-Tech" complex on one side, the "Business Park" on the other. An American flag fronts a professional building brick-framed on a football field slab. The flag looks like it's being stretched on the rack. Plastic trash mounds the freeway guard fence, there's a groomed and preserved family cemetery, some stones weather-worn as teeth, beside a notice: "Rezoning Application." Further, large red sign on abandoned barn: "18+ ACRES for sale," the acres part bush-hogged, part beech gulch tangled, assassinated blackberry stems pave the clearing, so the walker treads a giving bed of nails. Toppled farm structures, comb-toothed beams, visually porous, viny; cardinals flick in and out their darkness. Bare hardwoods, gnarled mourners; in the crotch of one a miraculous fir grows, no visible sign of support. The air above is birdful where the cleared blackberries have been thrust against an ancient fir wall, multitudinous finches and sparrows hop, dart, chitter within the tangle. This wild line is at the lip of destruction. Just beyond, the colonial earthmovers await their time.

1970—Environmental Protection Agency established by law

December 3   **STREAMSIDE**

This grey day, scouting the streambed, collies nosing curiously after. Branna trots up to greet weimaraner and lab, who live downstream. Leaves and snails pave the rocky course of clear cold miniature rapids. Developers once changed Sinking Creek's course. Now it erosively S-curves through the property. One great landfall a few years ago created a straggled cliff, but also a weedheld streamside plateau, shoving the S toward the neighbors' sycamores. Here are weeds, tumbled riprap, baby boulders, composition stone, underground rockridges bared, all mossed—a place for stream sounds only. Underground springs' outflow pipes' mouths are dry. No twig moves. We could be here forever, tranquil, chill, and rise to a new season.

1901—Theodore Roosevelt's first annual message to Congress on conservation

December 4   **MULTI-USE FOREST**

Only a mockingbird, state bird of Tennessee, loyal despite cold, but fluttering on treetop next to food mart—covering its feathered back. Further on, the university woods, saved, apparently, for now, from student housing. The university itself roars and hums across the railroad tracks. Here in cold silence are towering labelled hardwoods—red oak, northern ash—and matchstick tumbles of salvage pines, felled first by southern pine bark beetle, then by saws. This is a multi-use forest: its trails were once a "Perrier parcourse" route with exercise stations now rotted away, but hence a trail bike race route, ROTC training ground, environmental art gallery, also dogwalk, running trail, assignation site. Multitudinous uses weigh on the side of conservation, since, if it is razed, the trees and human uses are cut off at the root.

1952—"Killer Fog" in London (to Dec. 8)

December 5   **FROZEN EARTH**

Dawn, 21 degrees, surface earth solid now, all moisture frozen, leaves seem dry. Released collies exult, race ahead, tails plumed. Faye tightwires a trunk. Their vacuum cleaner canister drinksite all ice. Even the deer spoor, nosed, is frozen. Crow and vulture weather in the air, while all other life seems sunk another dimension down. This frozen earth is significant as the leaf-fall, like a seal on temperate nature's contract with this life. Sunrise as we cross Dead Man's Pass makes solitary swinging leaves glow and the convergent streams, for a bare moment, golden.

1905—Teddy Roosevelt recommends establishment of a bison preserve

Sinking Creek Journal

December 6   **DEEP RIVER**

    A-1 Auto Salvage next to Judgment House: Tour Your Final Destination; spruce ranchettes, decaying trailer, burnt chimneys, rusting one-lane cantilever bridge . . . River Ridge Campground down on the Holston, totally abandoned, coldest day of the year: ambiguous wooden structures, picnic tables, the dinghy Frances Anne half-buried in the earth. The Holston swift, very swift, dark green, deep, loamy pebbled sand. Snags reach out, jut; other side, a hundred-foot stone cliff, a transmission tower tops it. As the white-lit rapids swirl, white tentacular embedded trees, slightly sinister, black crevasses, watercourse over them has formed icicles. They're still in shadow. Sinking Creek leads toward this spot, its rocky coastline rises as it sinks somewhere invisible. Somewhere near here it burrows to meet the Holston. Some H2O molecule that passed our door might be tumbling into it right now to enter, eventually, the Mississippi's miasmic delta.

1947—Everglades National Park established

December 7   **INCOMING SNOW**

    8:00—clear at dawn, cold, windless. 9:00—wind slightly rises. 10:00—billowed cloud fringe encapsules western horizon. 11:00—gusts roar pine tops now, low cumuli moving fast mottle the sky, make the sun dance. 12:00—cloud cover torn apart, open sky, wind shift WSW to NNE. 1:00—cloud cover pattern has changed, with large lumps of darker stratocumuli and wide gaps of sun. 2:00—entirely grey now, with even darker mass moving swiftly NE up the valley to us. First isolated flakes, dense-looking, more complex gusts, vulture swerves low, trainwhistle; nuthatch, Carolina wren, house finch all together on the sheltered feeder. 3:00—lighter, no snow, for a moment the sun is a silver dollar about to be palmed by an even darker cloudbank and ringed by a kettle of vultures. 4:00—snow thickens, blurs contours, salts collies. Japanese silvergrasses toss their heads. Night's visor is lowered.

"I'm from the South, will always be from the South. I'll never get used to snow—how slowly it comes down, how the world seems to slow down, how time slows, how age and sin and everything is buried. I don't mind the cold. The beauty is worth it." Rick Bass, **Winter** *(1991)*

December 8   **BRITTLE REALM**

Brittleness reigns, record-setting cold. Sprawling pokeberry stems and grapevines snap. Slaking feet crunch grass, its tiny frost prongs. The resilient parsley leaves are finally yellow; fennel, defeated, droops. White-rimed thyme leaves fall at the touch. Only rosemary is ever green. The frozen spider hangs balletically from its frozen web, even the crows perch side by side, as if reluctantly acknowledging the Power. Mourning doves, like a flock of monstrous sowbugs, cover and glean the seedfall, plucking seeds from ice. This is mild country in the world view, but our creation lives in the present, anticipation itself not even a cold comfort.

" . . . without the trees' bright mantle of snow, the world turned a dark, dark green, nearly black, with the gray shards of clouds hanging everywhere, the white of the snow still clinging to the ground. A black and white world. When I walked high enough I would be inside the clouds themselves, distance turning to ray nothingness, the rain beading directly onto my sodden clothes in tiny crystal spheres." Pete Fromm, **Indian Creek Chronicles** *(1993)*

December 9   **STONE WALL**

Steep treed slope across Sinking Creek Road from us. Until it was channelized, sheets of rainwater raced downhill across the road, (result of new construction high above), and doing what comes naturally eroded the stream's steep banks. Here, in warm weather, a poison ivy barrier punctured by tiger lillies; denuded now it clearly reveals, a few yards up, a freestone wall, erratic, partly sunken. For a long time this appeared to be abandoned pasture wall, since all this growth a century ago was yet unborn, and cattle, dinosaurlike, grazed these hills. But the neighbor says it is all that is left of a great mansion conflagrated when he was a kid, so hot he could feel it on his porch hundreds of yards away. What fabled mansion was this? Who

Sinking Creek Journal

would build such on this then dirt road? On the 1960s topo map it is there, a heavy black rectangle. The artifactual wall is much less impersonal, its nonlinear tumble comfortable, nature's terrain of caprice.

"There had always been a gigantic sycamore tree in Wilson's front yard. Flaxman had a tree surgeon to cut the top part out of it. He had hay stacked in the house. Right about that time, when he was tending to the sycamore, lightning struck the house, set it on fire, and burned it right down, all the way to the ground right quick." Dan Butterworth, **Waiting for Rain** *(1992)*

December 10   **CHAIR AMID LEAVES**

This old upholstered chair must have been in the forest for at least a quarter century. It reclines above the slope, other vine-covered undifferentiated forms around it. It is the color of the leaves but it is not the leaves. Every time you pass you notice it as *not* the leaves. It would take a power not of this world, or one deep-buried in the genes of insanity, to undifferentiate the constructed and the grown, not to notice the fatal mark of hands. And more so when its history is known: for this is where the neighbors' sons would take their girls, their poteen, and their guitars. Sultry summer evenings their bluegrass would emanate downhill, as though the hills themselves were plucking. Would it not be unnatural to deny this human history, to deanthropomorphize the chair amid the leaves?

1997—Julia Butterfly Hill ascends her redwood

December 11   **THE DEAD**

The last visit here was several years ago. Steep logfallen trail, off to left an ancient fence corner, more posts fallen now, more rusty barbed wire freed. Trees are tall, leaf-fall thick. Collies must think it queer to stop; they nose about. Orange tape circles the corner post, speaks a recent survey. Scuffing out the decaying leaves, one toppled stone plinth, then another. The three surviving buried headstones cleared: Samuel R. Haley, Husband of Matilda Haley, Born 1830, Died 1901; John Franklin Cole, Born January 20, 1840, Died May 18, 1916. Franklin McClatchey, Born

Fred Waage

July 4, 1883, Died June 25, 1901. Seven other stones there are, unlettered—perhaps children. This is the Bastian farmstead's southwest corner. The dead are twice buried in this forgotten corner. A forest has risen between their bones, blankets them softly each fall as ever their monuments sink slowly, year by year.

1997—Kyoto Protocol on CO^2 signed, not ratified by U.S.

December 12   **PASTURE AND WOODLAND**

Cirrus horsetails over Dry Creek Road, best known for drunken teens' totalled cars. Stretches of the creek are now whitely frosted over. Yesteryear's tobacco fields now sprout future Christmas trees, cornstubble barns are dying, falling to new-framed barns with Christmas wreaths, plastic deer, real shaggy ponies, satellite dishes; Tipton Pride barbecue sauce for sale here, goats for sale, hot green poinsettia-choked houses, custom collision repair beside the Tabernacle Baptist Church. Uphill, where light decked splitlevels overlook cow pastures, there's a whole ridgetop subdivision that's landed midfield like a Martian vehicle. Pastoral hollow, stream, endless haystack rolls, black cows with black calves—suddenly the National Forest hits, all evergreen, rhododendron and laurel, rising rocks, Laurels Campground built by the CCC. Across the road, a truckbed repository. There's no wide threshold here between pasture and woodland. You choose one or the other. Beech Cliff Freewill Baptist Church, deep nestled, high clapboard belfry, says it all: THE SHEPHERDS HEARD AN ANGEL AND FOUND THEIR LAMB.

"The orchards and truck farms that formed the historical matrix for already existing suburban garden cities would be uprooted and new development would coalesce into a shapeless amoebic mass." Mike Davis, **Ecology of Fear** *(1998)*

December 13   **SHELF FUNGI**

Walking the undifferentiated wet autumn woods, phenomena previously unnoticed leap to the consciousness, and attention seeks them out.

Sinking Creek Journal

Thus, sudden awareness—the white *pleurotus* fungi encircle two- or three-foot stumps all through the lower level woods. This bright shelving monumentalizes the anonymous stub whose substance it is breaking down. Like the snakeroot spires of spring, these play the human imagination like torches—or, contrarily, gravestones. Or as both—pyres. The eye imbibes, the imagination digests, unmediated sensation to verbal formulation, projected outward again, reformulated, acculturated. No one can deter this process—it is rooted in our cortex as *pleurotus* is in the trunk (there the mind goes again!). Is it worth all the reflection? But then, this reflection, this inward frenzy, is deep-rooted too. Let it be, the torches blaze, the monuments rise, the pyre fires leap. Overexamined life is not worth living anyway.

"On the ground little earth-tongue fungi stuck out their tongues; impudic phalloids ejaculated their spores; sidesaddle fungi, branched coral fungi, black fungi like tough truffles rose from the sodden earth. And everywhere the smell of mold spreading through the ground-water capillaries filled the grove with that venerable odor . . ." Donald Culross Peattie, **Flowering Earth** (1939)

December 14   **SHALE**

A warm week ahead, the melt has unleashed scents that tie collies' noses to the ground. Even the human can detect a richer odor rising. Unfrozen deer or bear spoor reveals much to those who are interested. Where the slope is steepest, softened soil has released its grip on limestone and shale plates. All shapes and sizes, they strew the ground like trashed crockery. If it rains before the next freeze, they will slide further down. There is no mother lode atop the ridge—they seem to emerge, high up, through spontaneous generation. This one shelters a cocooned grub. The rock is grey, roughly trapezoidal, shaped like a boat. It is undercut on its thickest side, fungally greened there. Its two deepest fissures support inch-long crops of moss. Breakage lines on another side suggest it broke off an extruded outcrop, but its softened contours suggest long residence in weatherbeaten solitude—or not really solitude, rather as the host, or homesite, of grub, fungus, and moss.

1955—Tappan Zee Bridge over Hudson River opens

December 15   **SINKHOLE**

Writing in a new building, organic tree-form art on the walls, a lunar landscape all about: bare earth, topped hills, boulders moving, pinstripe houses rising, artificial fountains in artificial lakes proudly spewing. Only the window-framed white-spired brick church has escaped these razors. Back the road a piece, though, amid strip malls, a deep sinkhole—a hundred feet across. The strip malls have tiptoed to its very edge, in fear recoiled. A tall red maple, deep-rooted at its bottom, pierces heavenward. This sinkhole has been here a long time. Water-carved limestone labyrinths entangle the underground whereon we construct. The church spire in-spires many, the maple spire, fewer, in its sinkhole cathedral, drawing up the heaven beneath our feet.

"In the rocks of the earth we can hold in our hands the crystals of nature's creative spirit, an elemental architecture of energies that have shaped our world since the beginning of time." Thomas Fairchild Sherman, **A Place on the Glacial Till** *(1997)*

December 16   **HUNTERS**

Blue pickup at top of our route, where the POSTED sign no longer hangs. The collies' jaws drop: "What is this?" It must have driven from the ridge's other side. Someone must have cleared again the old route up from Hickory Springs subdivision, abandoned since the ridge was zoned out of development. Tire tracks ahead—surveying another assault? No, all is clear around two turns, Faye abark. Completely motionless—half-reclined—orange helmets, flak-y jackets, rifles slanted—at first they appear like statues escaped from a Vietnam War memorial. They overlook the grassed green roadway cleared, spread, and seeded midwoods in September. The deer will come to graze and be hauled out in body bags. "Hey" they call, still unmoving, "hey!" Wave and urge collies onward; you can read anything from rage to friendliness in a "hey," but these guys have guns. Homeward bound, the collies seem subdued: "Whose forest is it anyhow?" They're more upset than their human—men have hunted, men

Sinking Creek Journal

will hunt. At least they're not gunning their unmuffled pickup through Washington County, polluting the air, polluting their bodies with Old Milwaukee and the roadsides with its slow-degrading containers.

1841—first recorded New Madrid earthquake

December 17 **SCENTS**

Orange-mottled pre-sunrise clouds, chill trails now despite expected record heat. Pileated woodpecker calling. New parallel lines of stride-separated disturbance in the leaf cover call collies' attention. Lines too far apart to be vehicular. Stalker Tom Brown would instantly identify their perpetrator; it's hard to imagine two black bears in such tandem scuffling for mast. It's easier to imagine two slop-footed hunters wearing big boots, but hard to imagine hunters leaving such nostrilfuls of their presence. The collies, nonetheless, with their olfactory memories, seem to feel we've entered an unwonted human zone. And lo, the hunters have left their spoor—a pile of corn. They're nothing if not persistent, despite no evidence of any kills. It's amusing to imagine chuckling wild turkeys beak-scuffling the leaves as the departing pickup disperses exhaust where they tread. At Dead Man's Pass, heading back, the clouds above have whitened and sun suggests it's about to peer over the shoulder of Buffalo Mountain.

"*. . . I clambered down the steep stream*
Some forty feet, and found in the midst of bush-oak and laurel,
Hung like a bird's nest on the precipice brink a small hidden clearing,
Grass and a shallow pool. But all about there were bones
    lying in the grass, clean bones and stinking bones,
Antlers and bones: I understood that the place was a refuge for wounded
    deer; there are so many
Hurt ones escape the hunters and limp away to lie hidden; here they
    have water for the awful thirst
    And peace to die in . . ."
    Robinson Jeffers, "The Deer Lay Down their Bones" (1954)

December 18   **WINTER LIVES**

Brush Creek parallels Sinking Creek, but stays above ground until it reaches the Holston. Its underground passage is through the city's perpetually dying downtown, where during floods it raises manhole covers in wrath. Out here on Brush Creek Road it flows 'cross the railroad, down behind rusted houses whose porches sag under dead refrigerators, fusty pig lots, gaping dead brick factories, sycamores twisted grotesquely with strange fruit. This is an avenue of desperate survival, of trucks without wheels. Periodic signs: "Impassible During High Water: Travel at Own Risk." They tell its life story. Every few plots are piled dead cars. Sun glints unnaturally off a high hill—not Oz, but an auto graveyard suspended in air, amid trees. Suddenly appears a single green engine on the tracks, surreally generic, labelled EAST TENNESSEE RAILROAD, backing forward a single black tank car, a trainman hanging, impassive, surveying with stoic surmise this landscape of winter lives.

"If we are fascinated by the statistics of magnitude, we are no less fascinated by the statistics of our insignificance."
Wendell Berry, **The Unsettling of America** (1977)

December 19   **ENCOMPASSING GREYNESS**

Air is grey, smells of rain. Chill haze blurs vision. Sky nearly as dark as bare trees' branches; birds dance among them nonetheless, the red-bellied woodpecker hops to a trunk, tufted titmouse lets go its disconcertingly loud call. Runners on Sinking Creek Road appear to swim somnabulistically, crows pass above with silent purpose. Branna makes no forays at the opposing dogforces, but noses upstream and downstream, as though seeking something. The "pathetic fallacy" is fallacy only in a very deep sense. Nature is the agent, and sinks its unverbalizable moods deep into us humans. The red-bellied woodpecker cares not a whit about it, but this encompassing greyness blesses and ensorcells the human spirit.

1913—Raker Act authorizes Hetch Hetchy Dam after a ten-year battle

December 20   **BAD RAIN**

It is raining from a clear sky. Dense pre-dawn fog has condensed as air warms, on limbs and persistent leaves high above; droplet weight grows and the droplets hit the leaf-covered ground, all over the slope. No wonder the leaf mould increases so fast through the winter, the leaves losing form and shape, elementally disintegrating to feed trout lily roots. So really when it is not too cold or too warm, and humidity is high, rain falls in the forest from winter unto spring. All is not lillies though: it may be contended that fog condensation traps particulate pollution, "cleansing" the air but "dirtying" the ground. More highly documented is the entrapment of chemical pollutants, endangering the lives and health of humans (Donora, London), and plants, particularly bryophytes, and trees, their often hosts, themselves. Mosses capture and soil-bind nutrients in atmospheric precipitation. The human hand poisons this nutritive cycle. Hence the irony in figurative fog: "fog" is confusion, disorientation, mental impairment. "Fog" poisoned by anthropocentric figuration lives in our language, a toxic parasite.

1951—first atomic-powered electric generator

December 21   **LIGHT POLLUTION**

7:22 PM—Winter Equinox this year. Illusory darkness. Dog messaging throughout the valley. Warm and still. Black branches against a totally grey sky. And why is the grey sky visible, how can it still backdrop silhouettes? Even in this narrow cleft backed by a mountain, human-generated light bleeds over the western hill, reflects to us off clouds. Ironic that we illuminate the darkest moment of the year, as though to deny, yet again, nature's seasonal powers. Consider: night light is reflected off the particulates that are airborne byproducts of the power generation that enables the night light. A perfect cycle of energy waste and habitat invasion. Its motivation, one might speculate, an overwhelming species-wide fear of the dark.

1928—Congress approves construction of Boulder (Hoover) Dam

December 22   **VISITOR**

After some holdout, strong rain falls, pencil-points on skin. Half-dark, the Visitor arrives. The Visitor is a city human, and environmentalist. The Visitor is led through gardens, along creekside, and up to Dead Man's Pass. It is interesting to re-observe an adoptively native place through a Visitor's eyes—one can feel how imperceptibly the lived space has been domesticated, a gloss of familiarity smoothing it, as nacre around a jagged sand-grain. Of course, such a gloss is adaptational necessity for any organism. None can be a Permanent Visitor. Perhaps our Visitor's astonishment does not express any "truer" unvarnished perception of the place. Perhaps the varnish itself is Place.

*1975—Environmental Policy and Conservation
Act establishes strategic oil reserves*

December 2   **REALM OF ROOTS AND STREAMS**

"We ain't in Kansas any more," jokes the Visitor. "Or maybe, worse, this *is* Kansas." The Visitor is looking for coffeehouses. Meanwhile, the rain has passed, the clouds are breaking, droplets hang from every sprig of rosemary. The trail-in-progress along the Nameless Stream is almost untraceable, wet leaf layers. Moisture has enhanced mossy cliff face's green, darkened, seemingly, the black cave mouth. Captured Sinking Creek Springs gush from pipe mouth strong and cold as ever. Despite the years, the root mass of fallen sycamore, twelve feet across, still presents a solid earth wall; between it and the steep slope only the stream course is visible, and we aren't even on Sinking Creek anymore, rather we are Visitors to a realm of roots and streams where there are no names.

*1938—Long-thought extinct deepwater fish, the
coelecanth, caught off South African coast*

December 24   **INVADERS?**

While most shrubs have died back or browned out, the multiflora rose canes remain green all winter, eager and ready to be first off the line when tolerable warmth arrives, and to tear at the coats of humans and beasts.

Sinking Creek Journal

They've settled in to take over all the property's hedgerows, creating their own thickets of defense. You can find their invasion in microcosm here, as even the giant ragweed cannot pierce its cover. Multiflora roses were brought to the U.S. a decade before kudzu—another offender with original good intentions, fortunately unadapted to this shady valley—and later than the Japanese honeysuckle still entwining the telephone pole. Contemplation of these sweet thieves questions the term "invasive" and its premise of bioregional differentiation. Take it back far enough and Earth's original organic life constitutes invasive species, invading the third rock from the sun as it cooled. Or, viewed another way, opportunistic invaders are nature's venture capitalists or its Wal-Marts—totalizing monocultures. Less theoretically, they'll all be cut back before spring.

1893—Henry Ford completes his first successful gasoline engine

December 25   **CULTURE'S WRAPPINGS**

Oasis of warmth and sun. Fleeting clouds, the vultures fly high. A human catharsis, as of ritual, vibrates unseen in the air. There is a retreat to dwellings and vehicles cluster before façades, like piglets at the teat. Beasts are mainly silent, human voices rise, almost a chorus. Every day, not just today, the gift of life is given, mutually, to each living organism. Survival's elements are provided naked and unwrapped. Culture's wrappings are gifts to itself, of necessity the forgetting human culture is but an afterthought, tucked in a corner of nature's great mutuality. On the porch rail, the song sparrow opens its throat.

"The Fo'castle, being low and strongly built, stood solid as a rock, but its walls thrummed in the gale. I could feel the vibration in the bricks of the chimney, and the dune beneath the house trembled incessantly with the onslaught of the surf." Henry Beston, **The Outermost House** *(1928)*

December 26   **STORMS**

High wind tears ice-cold rain pellets. House finches crowd on the feeder like humans at Starbuck's. The pellet-rain strikes red barns, where hock-deep calves bend to the trough. Further out, in mud, black cattle graze unblown and stoic. Black-bearded imprudent waterproofed running human passes pool beneath the bridge, great blue heron rises, strokes deeply downstream. A storm within the body too, aching, invasive organisms as natural to it as the cold rain. Microscopic beetles gnaw the body's trunk. These are not fatal dis-eases; in fact, they bespeak an almost aesthetic harmony. Tonight there will be snow and fevers will break.

> "We are vulnerable because of our very intricacy and complexity. We are systems of mechanisms, subject to all the small disturbances, tiny monkey wrenches, that can, in the end, produce the wracking and unhinging of interminable chains of coordinated, meticulously timed interaction." Lewis Thomas, **The Medusa and the Snail** (1979)

December 27   *Workbreath*

Emerging sun glints Buffalo Mountain's snowy high-ridged forest, while all is clear and briskly cold down here. Along Cherokee Road, scene from a 50's children's book: brick condo frames, tinkertoy rectangular rise, men are nailing, wheelbarrowing, digging. Their hot condensed workbreath clouds the site. Fire glows in a barrel. Further back, men are also working at "Winwood Estates," right now a line of cinder block boxes burrowed into a former gulch filled last summer with golden mullein torches; now netting supports lightstarved grass sculptured down a slope of artifice. One wonders how the dead-end householders, above this project, their residences now nakedly revealed, feel looking down into these hanky "estates." Home sweet home indeed.

1977—Clean Water Act passed

December 28   **HAWK**

Seed-eaters, desperate, flurry—more than just because a human opened a door. A much larger bird flies up onto the black chestnut, its off-white breast: a red-tailed hawk, poised a few seconds, then arrow flight, sharp veers, almost a full circle around the apartment, accelerating . . .

Sinking Creek Journal

a force breaks the domestic backyard's invisible plane . . . they drop sometimes . . . a seconds' visit . . . cardinal once crashed a window . . . outdoors just in time to see it rapt away by this force . . . tangled leafless limb striations camouflage the hawk perfectly . . . red-brown and streaked on back, a node of total awareness . . . the human mind weak in the shadow of its wings . . .

1973—Endangered Species Act passed

December 29   **GUNFIRE**

Climbing the ridge, collies seem over-alert, staring ahead, glancing back, fixing that famous gaze. A bit onward, still relatively low—the answer: it appears at first that the hunters have come closer. A blue pickup, end of another petered-out access road, seems to have been purposely concealed. As usual, Faye disappears ahead. Where she's gone, concussive shotgun blasts; a call for her, panicking, hear her frenzied barks, now she's coursing back. Her unarmed human, weaponless, dressed in green, is really as helpless as a deer. No alternative save retreat. How easily guns can conquer the woods . . . an hour later smoke rises dark yellow from the crease where the hunters must have been. Did they set it? 911 knows. Will it spread? Fire and gun-fire. Nothing, no one, is safe.

1970—Occupational Health and Safety Act (OSHA) signed into law

December 30   **POWER SAW**

All afternoon, while shadows lengthen northeastward, the power saw buzz rises to orgasm, falls, rises again. Apparently the wielder is over the valley, up the facing hillside, behind a house that fronts Strawberry Lane. Strawberry Lane was forged in the 1980s along a wooded ridge. Its lots were auctioned, the attendees received a free yardstick, courtesy of the auctioneer—worthy symbol to section the earth. To his credit, the householder in question hand-built his blue house, but apparently twenty plus years are plenty of time to grow the foliage which must now be excised.

Fred Waage

Between the power saw's climaxes fallen limbs clatter; must be a whole copse or grove they're slicing out. In fact, squint and you can see trunks severed, low naked branches pulled down, but not the pulling hands. Since humans first became agriculturists, the collective hand has been pulling down its former residence. But try as it will, no hand can uproot the ingrown memory.

1854—the U.S.'s first oil company, Pennsylvania Rock Oil Company, founded by George Bissell and Jonathan Eveleth

December 31   **SKYSCAPES**

It is scarcely light. The landscape is dark blue. Strange colors invade the sky. First, to the west, round clouds are orange, sky robin's-egg blue, overwrought blue—a Disney movie sky; then, through eastern trees, spear-shaped pineapple-colored clouds shaped like anger—or, rather, a hawk's bill, and in a moment, a moth's wing, torn to shreds. This day, this place, is waiting on rainstorms, sky aberrancies, alphabets of meaning to those creatures literate in the language of natural forms. For how long did our protoparents have no need to articulate, how long was the indicated cloud or tree a glyph in a far yet intimate language? Returning, the real sunrise—a sheet of light both silver and gold, platter of the gods.

1970—President Nixon signs the National Air Quality Control Act

January 1   **PICKUP HABITAT**

Wildlife has not noticed the passing of a human year, only the passing of last night's rain. Trail wheelruts are full, as is the vacuum canister the collies drink from. Up there, however, we find blue pickup #1 again. Orange warning sign on its windshield: obviously marks a free-fire zone. Faye appears dubious, so we retrace our pawmarks. Hidden in the brush, as before, blue pickup #2. Required mode of transport for all Tennessee hunters? Move up on it, find window open, hood and engine burned out, black, skeletal, crumpled. Of course, this is nothing new. Dead vehicles fill woods around here. Some, surely, are hidden evidence. Rusted down, this one's excellent shelter and habitat—wasp and rodent clans climbing up for bittersweet and muscadine.

1970—National Environmental Protection Act (NEPA) signed

January 2   **INTERMITTENT STREAM**

The Bastian farmstead's home clearing seems to have been funnel-shaped, widest at ridge peak, converging downhill, the apple orchard, then the wood road out. At this narrowed terminus the intermittent stream begins. Intermittent, but more technically ephemeral—flowing only after heavy rainfall or snowmelt. Twenty-five years ago, clearing not much grown over, it was much less ephemeral, flooding the trail, its own baby valley jump-wide, fern-lined. Slow revegetation, more rainfall absorption, less flow. Now its course is a dead snake here. Not so, as we find, bouldering along it lower down. Seepage from the soil it passes through starts it pooling, running again, four-inch waterfalls, six-inch pools, mossy rocks overloom. Maidenhair and lady fern crowd its moist sides. Its wandering course irrigates afar. Such intermittent and ephemeral streams as this are essential to the lives of watersheds, have their own flora and microfauna, tribute nutrients into permanent streams, as this one does into the Nameless Stream, as spring seepage into our bog garden. This ephemeral stream may be subject now only to the vagaries of organic growth, but in general such streams are truly subject to extinction by any human construction, ORV passage, roadbuilding, living a thousand lives, dying a thousand deaths, always awaiting the final one.

1882—John D. Rockefeller establishes the Standard Oil Trust

January 3   **CLEARANCE**

Mirabile dictu. What we encountered on January first seems to have been the last hunt. Frost sparkles fakely on the holly, but as we mount upward acrid burning woodsmoke intensifies, then the sound of violent treefall, exhaust smog, gears grinding and thrashing. Warning red ribbons tied all 'round the old oak trees post limits of something bad being done to the earth. When we reach the farmstead, it is devastated land, in the center a pile of shattered trees burning, leaping flames, a bush hog backing mudruts where our trail turns downhill. The farm is being cleared once more. The intermittent stream will be less mittent now, for sure. We stand amazed at how quickly the foliage we took for granted can be annihilated. Bonfire in the boneyard should not evoke shock, awe, and grief—we know well it is one bonfire of many in the widening gyre. When first met, this space was just growing out of its previous clearance. This clearance now is too absolute to be agricultural. Call our field office of the Tennessee Department of Environment and Conservation; says, well, deed restrictions aside, you can log your own property, unless it is a water source, might cause pollution—it is a watershed: the intermittent stream—right, well, we'll look at it, see if there are any violations. . . . Directions to it? Directions? No directions will restore the trees.

1961—Idaho Falls nuclear reactor leaks, killing three

January 4 **DEAD TREES**

And then there are other complexities in deforestation. The dethroned Christmas tree being deported now was grown on a tree farm in North Carolina. Presumably the purpose of the tree farm was to grow trees to be cut down, and presumably the farm lives on land which was itself forested before being cleared to support arboriculture. We have been displaying a dead tree in the house for two weeks, as have millions of other humans. Is there a qualitative difference between the deadness of this tree and those on the Bastian pyre? Does intentionality or use create such a difference? What of all the unbought trees lying about the lot on December 24? Will they go to the pyre or to the chipper? Why can the trees of the mountain not at least be mulched, returned, however prematurely and whatever form, to the earth upon which they would, if not denied life now, eventually fall? At least our own killed tree is laid reverently beside several previous years' progressively skeletal ones, amid the rack of downed tree limbs, sapling, weed tangle, the unkempt forsythia patronizing all. Late afternoon the seedeaters threading this jungle eye it curiously and, one

Sinking Creek Journal

fantasizes, with appreciation, sort of as would be eyed a new youth center in the ghetto.

" . . . I do not think it too remote that we may come to regard the Earth, as some have suggested, as one organism, of which Mankind is a functional part—the mind perhaps: different from the rest of nature, but different as a man's brain is from his lungs."
Christopher Stone, **Should Trees Have Standing?** (1974)

January 5   CROWS SEEK MEANING

Hot January—65 degrees. Watercress spreads, bindweed shows purple. Rainfall gap. Collies sip water from caterpillar treads, leaves are ground to mud. Ginger wonders if the dormant lady slippers have been obliterated. Large murder of crows rises and wheels, crying out above the Bastian gravesite, its fallen limbs cleared, its crucifix still mutilated. The crows seek meaning. We trudge through viscous mud. Smoke haloes the pile of braised and incinerated trees, firetongues flick from a miniature volcanic ash dome. Leif bathes himself in muddy wheel ruts. The collies are all hot enough to lie in the Nameless Stream, inhaling water—they haven't done this since last summer.

1905—*President Roosevelt recommends establishing a bison preserve*

January 6   THAW

Unfortunately, less unseasonable warmth allows winter garden weeding. Hands in earth, galaxy of dark but consoling scents. By the bog, native horsetails continue to spread. Ant colony surprisingly active under a stone. Following bindweed's rhizomic spread, ultimate futility in uprooting the green fuse. Wild strawberries, likewise, telegraph tendrils across the hosta border, the tansy rough and still green. Branna and Faye wander and nose; Faye helps by digging up roots. Leif follows, weedpile to weedpile, stares meaningfully at his ubiquitous tennis ball. There are cicada carapaces, clustered, detailed and translucent *maquettes*. Weed roots mat decay, create their own loam beneath the decorative stones, mats which will recreate themselves in spring. A McDonald's rush on the feeders; sparrows, doves, wrens scuffle fallen husks. The railing cat scratches, a tuft of fur floats off like a massive snowflake.

1973—oil tanker grounded off Shetlands releases 80,000 tons of crude

January 7   **ECOCHAIN**

Dead officers have been asked to re-enlist. Dead vodka bottle bobbles in stream scum. Dead soccer ball on the opposing side waits. Dead milk carton sysiphusian, doomed to rise and fall forever in snag backwater. But any human who's lived long with a stream knows it is forever changing—course, banks, vegetation, geology. Lift a stone, dislodge a sycamore leaf, downstream the leaf impaled by twigs, rain (as now) starts to fall, the stream spreads, floats leaves off banks, soon they join the first leaf, mat together, twigs, small branches jam them, water flow is diverted to least resistance, over a horizontal stone, tiny rapids thereby created, rough water pebble by pebble eats at the opposite shore. In the barren winter, stream inscribes its history even as it changes. Like history, the gesture of a hand can shift it; like history, no hand can control the ecochain unleashed by that initiating gesture; like history, it leaves its castoffs on the shore or suspended in torment forever. Dead officers have been asked to re-enlist.

1953—President Truman announces development of an H-Bomb

January 8   **INFORMAL**

After great rain, an informal feeling comes. White pine heads explode in motion like bombs, vultures kettle dramatic and erratic in the beaks of the wind, incessant wind-tunnel howl, down the valley orange streaks never quite escape the horizon. A shotgun explodes, the rooftop drums. Dawn: sharp clear wind gusts. Sinking Creek has lost yesterday's contours; vodka bottle and little snags are gone. Lady Gravity's mission. On land, mud has hardened. Cats pace the gardens, tails raised. Red manx rubs jowl on a pruned fennel stalk.

Sinking Creek Journal

1863—ground broken in Sacramento for transcontinental railroad

January 9   **THE PICTURESQUE**

"Seen any snow yet?"—elderly man, cane, youth in his eye. Low grey sky, yet human spirits seem excited by a return to the relative discomfort of the normal, seem made garrulous by relief. Soon it comes in whiteout waves, fat and furious, exalting conifers, peaking like sugar on premature dogwood blossoms, enlightening earthmovers' bare gouges. Grabbing snowdays, schools close immediately. The ground itself is so warm crusty ridges pattern uncovered grass. Uphill each horizontal stone ridge is now highlighted behind the vertical trunks, an ice-imprisoned landscape, yet freed from sharp lines, a trifle, really, a look back. Goldfinches shake white echinacia heads, collies' black backs are salted, the male cardinals fluff their breasts, seeking the picturesque.

1908—Muir Woods National Monument established

January 10   **SURFACE AND CORRIDOR**

We follow a deer-trail to the ridge top; the valley dwellings now appear almost directly below us, and those of the opposite ridge—invisible from valley floor—unveil themselves, wide windows sunrise-gilded. You can tell by its residual width, careful placement upside the boulder ridges, careful low-incline curve over the shoulder of the ridge, that the trail is of human creation, hunters' access or logging trail (maybe itself constructed on a preexistent animal route). In barren times or, as today, ciaroscuroed over by a light snowfall, a discerning eye can detect, from above, tangles of such vestigial trails, merging, deadending, traffic multicorridors to high safety. Descending again, the human becomes a swinger from beech to beech, startling collies who thrive on order and replication. Now at last with "measurable" snowfall, the hunters of Appalachia, tracing spoor, can roam widely, it is the season of revelation for unclaimed human skeletons and corpses. The crimes of summer lie revealed, the thaw's foot and paw falls become molds. On this property, a week of warm collie cavorting has implanted so many, casts could be made in them. Every earth surface irregularity is imprisoned, fabulous cities, intricate iceline basketry, heelprint rubble replicates microarchaeology of entire lost civilizations.

1901—Spindletop, first Texas oil strike

January 11   **ST. FRANCIS**

Blown snow outlines St. Francis cupping a bird, blessing the shade garden. St. Francis was here before there were gardens to bless. Now, perhaps most pagan of Christian luminaries, he shares place with the Buddha, perhaps most Christian of pagans. Francis was here first, however, and over the years he has grown ever greener; now he is entirely moss except for the white face beneath his hood. St. Francis is also broken: a tree limb severed him at the waist, but he fits together so well that no one notices his breakage, as few notice his Earth's. St. Francis's Mother Earth, according to his *Canticle of Creatures*, "sustains and guides our life." In 1979 Pope Paul designated St. Francis as Patron Saint of the Environment. For St. Francis, an offence against creatures was an offence against the Creator—strongest defense of creatures his century would allow. Now in the 21st century, how to defend the creatures if you believe creatures and Creator are one?

1887—Aldo Leopold born

January 12   **OVERGROWN CLEARING**

Air has warmed, earth softened, snow is gone. Great Blue rises from the creek and veers off toward the Holston. Despite the weather, that pile of burned trees up there still smokes softly. Trying to navigate an alternative route, dump to ridgetop. In 1980 this was a clear cart track bordering a rectangular fallow field amid forest. The field's high point offered a view away to Sinking Creek's northwest ridge. A quarter-century later it is a nigh-impenetrable mixed conifer forest, the only view one of entangled deadfalls. Ground pine covers much of the former cart track and summer's rapturous poison ivy makes it toxic to humans. The pines have risen, been uprooted, new ones have risen; only the eyes of the mind can see the clearing as it once was. So there is a fine anticipatory revenge. Once the hand neglects the scythe, all is lost—or found—again.

1971—Ralph Nader forms Earth Action Group

January 13   **MOMENT IN FLUID TIME**

Domocentric day. Warm. Garlic is nippin'. Sun is reluctant to decline, throws up grey cloud bars like those on Erick's Army uniform. As light fades, rank increases. Now it is all grey. Many road walkers in the gloaming, the evening bark follows their progress. One of them bends to pick up debris from our frontage. The shame! Delinquent postal cars, rooflights flashing, drive upstream, and pizza-capped pickups, downstream. Gnats. Black hawk rustles into white pinetop for the night. Surging huskies pull their people by. Leif and Branna ritually bark at them. The huskies have changed over the years—whelped, aged, died—their human couple seems just the same. Urge: try to catch the moment in fluid time, when darkness truly seems inevitable—first lamp, last vulture—there is no duration, an unendingly unfurling wave only of which here, as everywhere, humans live in denial.

1921—U.S. Census Bureau reports 51% of citizens
live in towns of over 2,500 population

January 14   **BELL**

High in the forest, entangling the pileated woodpecker's raucous cry, invisible Berea Church's 10:00 service bell reverberates as clear as a—bell. Momentary fantasy figures a dialogue of summonses—where to go to worship—and a corollary: need it be a choice? A topozone map, 1960s no doubt, since it shows the "new" golf course, but no fourlanes, inscribes this thought. One four kilometer quad: four churches, four cemeteries. Berea Free Will Baptist was the center of the Sinking Creek community when its topographical isolation made it a *de facto* village beyond the city, buried in the valley. Beside the church were a schoolhouse and store—but no saloon. Presumably one could, before regrowth, stand upon the 2000' knob we climb and see the whitewashed cupola. But then the woodpecker's call would have rung down from a higher upland. The Call of the Wild, the Call of the Word, entangled throughout the white history of America. The bell on the church in the city on the hill. The Saved have no guarantee of perseverance. Every moment they are Free to Fall. Cannot this be also an environmental paradigm?

1972—plans announced for first U.S. nuclear breeder reactor

January 15   **CRADLE OF WARMTH**

Diffused sun, grey cloudcover, hot on the skin. This freestone garden is full of bugs, mid-January. Four raised beds connected by a stone terrace, laid on thick weedproof plastic ground cover, admittedly a technological intervention. Every fissure in it nonetheless weedchoked. Each stone lifted shelters a dense, minute root webwork, seemingly ungrounded, like an autonomous bundle of nerves, yet sprouting leaves. Among them spiders scurry. Under the raised-bed leaves and wall stones are small centipedes, ant colonies. A ladybug heats briefly on a rock. This is a hard cradle of warmth, self-radiating absorbed heat. Only the lambs' ears are soft; only they and the waiting lavender are green. Gamine, the garden cat, stalks the court approvingly, purely an inspection tour, no field mice in sight.

1919—Boston molasses spill disaster kills 21

January 16   **REFORESTING**

The wedge of our property east of the creek has been half mown and half left to reforest. Each year there are changes, but now unvegetated, the wilding portion's defects are revealed. Last spring an old maple fell, its aslant trunk becoming the area's gateway, but the progressing saplings are honeysuckle-choked and one charismatic multiflora rosebush seeks to capture all the birthing forest's energy. Hosts of ragweed still inhabit its hot center, but surely as shade increases their number will diminish. The sprucely lawned neighbor has not yet complained about this forest insurgency. Our durable willow still guards the wedge's point, as it has ever since its overarcher elm yellowed to a giant skeleton from Dutch Elm Disease in 1982. The pathwalker in this evolving wood can look across Sinking Creek, and under its bushy brows see his own house, garden, wheelbarrow, benches, dog toys—and a moment be a stranger, his very own Grendel.

1868—William Davis receives first (railroad) refrigerator car patent

January 17   **TREE FALL**

Supposedly, in temperate (versus tropical) zones, dark tree cover warms earth, counteracting any CO^2 reduction increased tree cover might effect. If this claim is sustainable, one global rationale for reforestation is likewise unsustainable, and more arguable and traditional ones, like preserving species diversity by preventing habitat alteration, return to the fore. And then there is, of course, sport: hunting organizations increasingly oppose industrial habitat destruction. You can reflect on these things trudging up to the farmstead, scene of the Last Hunt, scenting carbonic exhaust, hearing the bulldozer roar and scrape, viewing more newly-felled tall trees. They can surely not be pyred for burning without being cut up. Other human actors besides the cryptic dozerman will have to enter the scene, or he will need a very big saw. But in the disappearing shadow of the initial premise above, what harm has really been done by these trees' fall? The surrounding woods is dark and deep, its seasonal shade but reinforces the effects of the bulldozer's belch. Let's hear it for barren ground!

2007—Union of Concerned Scientists' nuclear clock reset
to 5 minutes before midnight due to nuclear tests

January 18   **CAT PREDATION**

Tam Lin, the red manx, has come home bitten all over, feverish, his throat and upper chest defurred. Four days and $300 later, he returns from the vet, plaintive, bald; immediately released into house arrest, he evades, leaps a window, arrows toward the hillside, a destination clear. Human screams follow. "Probably another cat," the vet had said. Nope. Tam Lin's off across the Nameless Stream, to Dead Man's Pass cliffs, the cubist low-ceilinged yet depthless cave, a traditional woodchuck homestead. Years agone the deceased dog Odin killed a pair living there, their bones strewed the yard for months. More recently, others muted Tam Lin's manx predecessor Sans. Lacking two toes he returned in midsummer for revenge. Never recovered, his rotting carcass scented the air. Now a reinactment is pending. For the family of manx—as often for the family of "man"—it's revenge or death. Tam Lin has vanished—he must be in the cave—then emerges again, precarious slope, scramble through barbed wire, over boulders, teeter on the edge, a grasp to the scruff, wade the stream. The cycle's thwarted. The cats (Mr. Ki earlier) clearly sought woodchuck young. The winter must be warm enough for reproduction. In predation and defense the domestication line blurs, constructions of control rendered false.

1733—Polar Bear first exhibited in U.S. (Boston)

January 19   **MAP AND ARTIFACT**

Through the bare trees, kudzu vine tangles, brief sun enlightens our city, its expanding topography spilling out of its high valley cup. The valley remains innocent in its primal lineaments, which go unperceived when the viewer is within the built environment. Chill, moisture-laden wind and roiling clouds, each sunbreak hits a different valley monument: church steeple, water tower, uphill 4-lane . . . like Nature's own Power-Point presentation. The valley strokes south west to a vanishing point, lower-built, more itself. The mind constructs its further course, imagines a map. There's little topography on the mind's map: a configuration of roadways and settlement symbols. The real valley melts like snow, revealing but the human stain. Is this rebuke or celebration? Or that the mind's creations, these thoughts, are themselves built artifacts?

1830—Webster-Hayne debates on the privatization
of Western public lands (to Jan. 27)

January 20   **NECROPOLIS**

Legend has it Farmer Bastian slept, when aged, every night in his coffin, so his neighbors would have but to lid it, bear it up the hill, and slide it into his vault beside his wife's. An elderly city lawyer swears this actually happened, that he was one of the pallbearers. The grave plot's blue picket gate stands open now, fallen timber cleared. Eastward, horses graze a frozen pasture. The twin cement vaults are chill, close to the sky: properly, this is a necropolis, earthspace ancient as humanity; the dead rest close to, commune with, whatever is Above. Farmer Bastian died in 1955 at 91, his wife in 1928, at 42. He had to wait a long time to lie with her. Beside the wire fence, rusted oil drums, piled bricks, an upturned grave marker as though cast away: FAITHFUL WIFE AND MOTHER, date indecipherable. A prior monument? A prior wife? A later wife? A wife cast away? Collies race the hard frozen mud wasteland. A new unburned tree pyre awaits the torch, a higher pyre of severed roots and two-foot trunks. This is the arboreal necropolis, conflagration/cremation, noun for the ashes.

"Everywhere you looked you could see the evidence of previous habitation, in the cellar holes of ruined farmhouses, in the isolated stone-lined wells, in the carefully constructed stone walls running through the pine woods and swamps, and in the fallen and dying barns, the numerous bottle dumps, and the rutted memory of old carriage roads. Something was alive amidst these ruins that could not be seen, there was a definite presence in the area." John Hanson Mitchell, **Ceremonial Time: Fifteen Thousand Years on One Square Mile (1984)**

January 21   **STOICISM**

Limbo—light rain perpetual, chill air, occasional gusts, damp dog-coats, dull colors, drifting mist entropic, towhees, white-crowned sparrows scratching seeds, wet pine needle webs, the persistence of a borderland between water and ice, rush and drum of half-frozen pellets, sanctimonious warmth, comfort framing reality, daring twilight power walkers like barren trunks practitioners of the stoic arts.

1954—Nautilus, *first nuclear submarine, launched at Groton, CT*

January 22   **CRABAPPLE**

Another day of mist and pinhead water drops. The trees embrace chill greyness in their arms, obfuscatory as politics. Different accents offset this monochrome; suddenly one sees whole the aged crabapple, pink each spring despite it all. But now, every intwisted limb all green, all milky green; *parmelia sucata*, cracked shield lichens, make its every surface cock petalic ears like Spring. This tree is green with age, seems turgid with fog, we might be underwater and the tree a great clump of sea moss, spread fingers to the tide.

1939—Uranium atom first split at Columbia U.

January 23   **ABANDONMENT**

32° all day, heavy grey above. Along Quarry Road, twisted limbs hang low over tarny Sinking Creek. Behind the juvenile detention center, the abandoned ovate stone quarries line up, flinty walls reach to blackness, sepulchres or basilicae abandoned by massive flinty Christs. Dead factory walls, loading docks, the road is crimped to a screen, turns, become the flaccid stub of an old highway. High-porched brick white-trimmed Victorians, cramped between old highway and new, facing factory, price reduced. Under the tardrop trestle, then the weedstrewn end of things.

"How alone is this house!—an unreeled
phone dangling down a hall
that never really could lead to tomorrow."
William Stafford, "Broken Home"

January 24   **LIMINAL**

Scaly plates, shagbark hickory and chinquapin, from midslope where the nut trees grow, now deep cold, shield no visible organisms. Even the hickory strips' lichen, so scarcely it clings to the mother tree, is black. These bark plates, undisturbed, eventually, continually, fall, seeding decay, feed the earth. Imagined insect eggsac, pupal shelters' redemptive falls, draw attention to that liminal space where roots and earth conjoin. This

Sinking Creek Journal

is the threshold for arboreal-dependent life. Mosses clustered there, low-crannied root tangles at the surface provide entry and shelter, also a vulnerable spot to begin predation on the tree. So many dead trunks are raddled at the base. So many severed, dead trunks then rot from within, their hollowness become rustic homesteads. Beetle-kill and saturated soil have felled whole white pines of a piece and opened a deep dark mouth toothed with stalactic rootlets, where any small creature may hide. Those fungi, ferns, wildflowers who thrive in specific microenvironments are vulnerable to, or profit from, this treefall and uprootment. How many endangered lady slippers have died since the southern pine bark beetle and southern bulldozer demolished the pines on whose roots they need to grow? Nothing green can stay.

1848—gold discovered at Sutter's Mill

January 25   **WHITE ROCK**

To the uninitiated, this would be a hidden neighborhood. This is the south side of Buffalo Mountain. From its summit here, White Rock falls blemished sheer; the first treetops appear tiny at its base. Snow is gusting, the road up narrow, sound-barriered freeway overpass, implacable rails, mooneyed goat and hunting hounds Unexpected road networks spread all along the slope, double-wides galore, defying gravity. W.B. Yeates (sic) Drive, Rilke Way—did a poet once tread here? All roads end below the rock: trash, abandoned foundation holes, redneck cliff-dwellers. Humans will fill every space, water in a sponge, the myth of fingerprints they spread, streetthreads beneath a rock, they find a hold and build on it. Here perhaps it is the strong mountain drawing them, transferring strength to weakness, granite empowering aluminum.

1905—Congress authorizes the first game preserve, Wichita Wildlife Refuge

January 26   **LIGHT**

In midday chill, a bright slant light sharpens every line. Wounded branch surfaces left by fallen limbs are white. Metallic power lines shine, the telephone pole is a cross of hope. Downward upcurving cucumber tree branches, so canopied in summer, are bright beckoning fingers. White socks Faye the collie has transported to the yard, scrap metal on the neighbor's trash heap, abandoned pumping station's tin roof plates, all flourish energy this brief cold prime. Humans, creatures of the light, we cannot control what it forces upon our sight. Do the blind also experience its presence, diverted through another sense not forbidden them?

1915—Congress establishes Rocky Mountain National Park

January 27   **ARCH**

Considering the arches, portals, thresholds through which a being may mythically pass into a new world or condition: the fringes beyond cultivation grow many of these, curved trajectories from frozen earth to frozen earth again. Against the cold monochrome these arches stand in bold relief. The more the eye searches them, the more it finds. Whitewashed red blackberry canes bending for the starting warmth to sound, a new plant spring from under the tip. The cat and rabbit can literally pass under these arches, the human in myth: to the regrowth of disturbed or deflowered land, desert to Eden in Jewish, Christian, American religion. Or passage to invasion, the road to empire. Himalayan blackberry (*rubus discolor*), evergreen blackberry (*rubus laciniatus*), like multiflora rose and many other species, follow the latter archetype literally, as humans do—invade, expropriate, and degrade native ecosystems. Millions and millions of *rubi* bend their canes the world over. This humble yard here on earth is, however, to our native *rubi* itself the invader. They bend perpetually to the task of reclamation, feeding as they do the very birds the human invader courts.

1888—National Geographic Society founded

January 28   **FROLIC ARCHITECTURE**

Snow finally sifts down, fine as flour. Every bract holds it, every unfallen deadhead. The sundial is an unreadable disc. Treeless patches on

Sinking Creek Journal

the mountainside stand out like ancient script. Snow clings to the fur of the roadside dead possum and the small dogs strident old ladies walk. For the first time this year human windshields must be scraped. Seed-eaters cluster under the overhang. Not yet enough to create frolic architecture, but enough to betray its potential to e-strange the dead flowerpot jungle, the unkempt brushpile, fractured rake, scattered mulchbags of seasons gone and yet to come.

1886—largest snowflakes on record (15" diameter) recorded in Montana

January 29   **SNOWY NOWHERE**

12°. Occasional snowflakes from passing clouds. Ironhard white pastures. Up in Spice Hollow, cattle cluster hay piles, horses stamp. "Cherokee Community Independent Freewill Baptist Church: It's 2007/Are You Ready for Heaven?" That doesn't sound too good. All the old farmhouse chimneys are smoking. Incongruous abandoned acid trip bus, and trampoline a dish of snow. Farm ponds frozen. Nowhere, under power towers, a fishing shop shaped like a Freewill Baptist Church neighbors a high graveyard, snow-filled plastic flowers beside every stone. Above, Buffalo Mountain, beyond the reach of condos and gated estates. But here, a slightly earlier point in human community's time on earth.

1927—Edward Abbey born

January 30   **WINDWHIPPED**

Every cloud has a silver lining. Unmoored yellow CAUTION banner whips the windshield. De-iced leaves dance the roadway like commercial animations, tipping complex formations, or suddenly vorticize up from a storm drain, the devil's horde unleashed. Every surveyor's flag flaps tinily, the green golf hole ones more largely, the patriotic one above the fast food restaurant larger still. Suburban trees that have been rolled are torches of glory. Conifers whip and display their needles' lighter-green backsides. Group excitement grips starlings and blackbirds, clouding and lineated on wires—over and over they dance. Mid-Appalachia writhes

Fred Waage

between two advancing air masses in almost erotic anticipation of the mastery to come.

> "Outside, everything has opened up. Winter clear-cuts and reseeds the easy way. Everywhere paths unclog . . . When the leaves fall the striptease is over; things stand mute and revealed. Everywhere skies extend, vistas deepen, walls become windows, doors open."
> Annie Dillard, **Pilgrim at Tinker Creek** (1974)*

January 31   **LINES AND SINEWS**

CAT—the earth-mover's clean lines and sinews—the hand, the forearm, the shoulder to the ground. The clean yellow movements of scooping, raising, lowering, squaring out cold barren ground for structures opulent, all the same postage-stamp ground, just like the already ones they face, the fountains of spontaneous artifice between. But the anthropomorphism is what attracts—industrial design—does anything non-digital take its primal form, its efficiency rationale, from a non-organic source? Can technology writ whole be essentially cut loose from this dependency, essentially be the Un-Natural? The Other? Can its instrumental, destructive proliferation be distinguished from species imbalance, naturally caused, destroying ecosystems? Locusts? Frogs?

1969—*Santa Barbara oil well blowout*

February 1   **DISAPPOINTMENT**

Culture anticipates snowfall. The charts quiver with anticipation. The thin red freeze line wavers back and forth, a live wire in time. Complex pollutants are spread on roadways, vehicles strategically parked. Liquor stores bloom like the cheeks of fresh young girls. It has been a hard winter in much of the country—cattle die and houses are crushed. Here the humans almost feel envy—cast aside by nature, left out of the action. Dawn brings no relief—bare earth, midday flurries—the freeze line drifts up the screen, by afternoon the earth and spirits are damp but there is no white to be seen. Vulture kettle fans out beneath grey sun.

Sinking Creek Journal

1992—Court in India declares ex-CEO of Union Carbide a fugitive from justice in Bhopal disaster

February 2   **Hoo**

Just before dawn: drizzle infused with smoke, moist and acrid. Loud voices cut through in argument. Flashing lights. Toward the forest, an undercurrent continuo hoo-hoo-hoo-hoo. Insistent. Listen. Silence. Hoo-hoo-hoo-hoo. Great horned owl. This is nesting season. Sounds like a male calling—fewer hoos. The O widens like visual migraine, encircles us, this land, the Earth, the universe. Think of all those rich squirrel nests waiting to be adopted. Screech owls are often heard on Sinking Creek, usually in late fall after dark, but no horned owls till now. Large predator is a good sign of eco-health: lots of small mammals for food. Potential food includes cats, however. Returning, the owl-hearer thinks the cats must be assembled and warned.

1954—President Eisenhower officially announces the first U.S. hydrogen bomb detonation—at Eniwetok Atoll in 1952

February 3   **Mad Music**

Dry and grainy snow grinding rockhard earth. Implacable wind roar fills the woods, penetrates every crevice. Rhododendron leaves hang, shriveled, frozen as despair. The collies dance—there seems to be no other life. The wind gusts the branches, aslant trunks, scrape and twang, high-pitched, a devilish bluegrass snowgreen dance. A decade ago such a driven windfreeze full of snow brought not discordant music but severed strings. Standing on the deck one might have heard the report and crash of pines, rhythmic to the popping of transformers. Now the rush is purely sterile of disaster, the music mads on.

1947—minus 63° centigrade, lowest recorded temperature in North America: Yukon Territory

February 4   **STEEP STREAM**

Upstream above Berea Church, Sinking Creek valley spreads out. Chestnut horse, white blaze, midfield, motionless in bitter wind. Treeline wanders fields where turkeys are shot in summer. In downstream view, descending funnel as hills converge into the cut where our house stands. Trailing further, the stream steepens, appears to emerge directly from snowy mountain wall. Up here chimney smoke, battened firewood, chained dogchorus, a new horse farm with gleaming sign "Seabiscuit Court" on the old McNeese farmstead bestrode by power lines. Sycamores fall back; all is hemlock and rhododendron. As you rise, wind dies, snowcover deepens, countless fallen whitecrusted trunks tangle over the streambed. We are entering the domain of hunters, ORV racers, oxycontin exchangers; Sinking Creek cuts east from the road, narrower, steeper; explorable to its very source once cold winds give way.

1987—Congress overrules President Reagan's veto of a clean water act

February 5   **DAZZLING BRIGHTNESS**

Yet one more day of dazzling brightness and piercing wind. Leif's tennis ball bounds high from the frozen ground. Nuthatches are alive on the cold shining sycamore trunks. Long-frozen daddy longlegs sprawled in a spiderweb dances ghoulishly with each gust. Abandoned pumping station collapsing tin roof clatters up and down. Stolid yuccas' bent leaftips vibrate metronomically. Wreaths of English ivy whip about. Torn clouds flow east. Single leaves toss erratically downward; they glint like foil. The hawk's shadow overcurves gleaming, tossing vegetation and a white-coated power walker, fellow predator.

" . . . I try to think of the winds as celestial music, as a sacred gift. They sculpted these dunes. They bring the rain and snow that nourish the grasses. They generate the lightning that produces cleansing fire. At night they rattle us from sleep, reminding us that we are enveloped in creative energy and that our home planet is spinning toward eternity."
Stephen Jones, **The Last Prairie: A Sandhills Journal** (2000)

February 6   **ANTICIPATION**

Early morning; a gibbous moon above wavelet clouds, streaks of purple in the west, orange glow in the east. By noon all is gray, by 2:00 desultory tentative flakes fall, gather, cease, gather again. Autumn-colored wren, towhee, hop among snow grains. All is atmosphere, no substance. Dump trucks, logloads, rumble. Human traffic fills the emptiness, illusion of a prelude. Hurry up, throw the ball, chorus the collies. Their anticipation is simple, unburdened by philosophy. Truth is in the nostrils.

1959—U.S. successfully testfires a Titan ICBM from Cape Canaveral

February 7   **SCENT AND THOUGHT**

Now warmer, surface earth is mud, paws can dance uphill where shod human foot slips. Pileated woodpecker booms all the way—its trees must be very hollow, or it's just exuberance at the thaw. Remains of a delicate curlicue ice sculpture in a deep wheel track. Collies form their nose-star position at a point undistinguishable to the human. Every new trip is on a different route to those whose senses have not atrophied. You can sense of how much biological and cultural evolution has deprived you—how unable you are to encounter the world in full sensory awareness, how much is cloaked under the dark cast of Thought.

1969—original Hetch Hetchy Dam powerhouse removed from service

February 8   **PAST TRAPPED**

An enclave—human community—one-story factory houses no bigger than their porches, its branching streets steadily lopped off by 4-lanes, strip malls, banks. Now there is only one street dead at each end across sullen Brush Creek, along the railway ... But stand in the middle of it and you are gone back fifty years—truck parts, abandoned hen coops, commodes lined up like a surrealist art exhibit, purple nightgowns, bedraggled paper dragons hanging, towel-padded tire swings, refrigerators on porches of refrigerator-sized houses. Everything is rusted, lived in, no disinfectant but sweat.

Fred Waage

*1887—Dawes Act passed: Native American tribal
land divided into individual allotments*

February 9   **ENCLAVE**

Less than a mile north, bordered upstream by condo complex, downstream by CSX railroad embankment, a widened cup, a covelet field. Here Sinking Creek takes on a new personality—wide, wandering, untreed, chortling over pebbles, not shouldering through rocks. The pebble riffles glint in the light. A barn, harrows, leantos; suburban cattle lounge and chew behind split-levels. So many farms have been enclosed, up-priced, developed over recent years, why has this stream-pierced circle of earth held its own. Who has the power to do ill yet done none?

1870—Congress establishes the U.S. Weather Bureau

February 10   **SPRING NOT SPRUNG**

Barren winter, the old pumping stations stands, more desolate and ugly than when it is a shunned summer shape and entirely cloaked in poison ivy. Now the vines wait, gripped to decay, the graffitied cinder block occasionally splotched by organ pipe shaped abandoned mud dauber nests. The torn up aluminum roof sheets await a new yellow jacket kingdom. Rusted, locked metal doorways are cold to touch, their skull-and-crossbones poison labels are long gone, as well as their chlorine. About twenty feet away, the encumbered spring enriches the Nameless Stream. Elders remember it as unhoused farmpond feeder, swimming site. Then came the municipal water system, the structures of control, the steel-topped cement shafts. This utility died when the water became too degraded to chlorinate, the rusted piping collapsed in a waterstorm. How lovely it would be to tear away all the superstructure, let the springflow create its own channels, invite back all the life that once surrounded it.

*"Throwaway landscapes . . . used to occur on the edges of settlement
everywhere. Richard Mabey, a British writer and naturalist, describes*

them as the 'unofficial countryside.' He uses the term for those ignominious, degraded, forgotten places that we have discarded, which serve nonetheless as habitats for a broad array of adaptable plants and animals: derelict railway land, ditchbanks, abandoned farms or bankrupt building sites, old gravel pits and factory yards, embankments, margins of landfills." Robert Michael Pyle, **The Thunder Tree** *(1993)*

February 11   **MAPLE BUSH**

Sheet ice rims the creek, its every tiny mossy backwater. Anonymous small-leafed greens creep up its slopes as well as living pachysandra donated two decades ago, presumed extinct. Low down riprap clefts, sun touching pine tops backhand, itself already below the ridge. Chickadees swarm in the maple bush, look like overripe fruit. . .the maple bush, once an overbearing tree, felled, sproutspray grows out the stump, regularly trimmed, makes a fan of leaves like the fiber frame of a leek flower.

1854—debut of coal gas street lighting

February 12   **SAWDUST AFTERNOON**

In Niger the Sahil sands are retreating to arable land, one sapling at a time. Earth no longer stripped for tillage, baby trees are rooted in compost holes. Their roots hold the soil, their detritus regenerates it. Another world from wooded still-temperate mountainous Appalachia, yet imagined as we weave through a rich cold forest filled with snags, wholesome scents of decay borne on fat rain-incipient air. Imagined on the stripped farmstead, a half dozen trunk-ated maples lying side by side, an ecoparody of the entombed farm couple uphill. Counting their rings—how many years of hydraulic effort have here been cut off in one sawdust afternoon. Oblique sawmarks disguise the truth, but perseverance reveals all these maples were over fifty. A half century in half an hour. What a midlife crisis.

1826—Creek Indian treaty renouncing all tribal lands signed

February 13   **OPENINGS**

 The telephone wire cut makes a downward plunge, open straight through the trees. Before spring the walker can plunge with it, avoiding kudzu, catching on the bare ground cleared by other shortcutters. When the warm bars of light cross it a couple of months from now, poison ivy and glory vines will have begun their rise, and pine saplings, broad oriental kudzu waves. The walker will hesitate, and take the long roadway's safe curves downhill. All winter cherrypicker assemblages have been pruning to keep these wires free. The full-sun vines, of course, would fail without this clearing—a strike against species diversity in a small space. Such openings go way back, historically enshrined, the work of fire, storm, or human hands.

"'It's a county road?' Doc asked.
'It's built for the benefit of certain companies that operate in this county, but it's not a county road, it's a state road. It's to help out the poor fellas that own the uranium mines and truck fleets and the marinas on Lake Powell, that's what it's for. They gotta eat too.'"
Edward Abbey, **The Monkey Wrench Gang** (1975)*

February 14   **ICE**

 Grey and cold, the mourning doves' grey coos a steady background—single coo, upnote, three more—a pattern incessant as breathing. Glistering sleet candies the herbage, crunches underfoot. Bare ice crust on a birdbath bends to the fingertip. Red drag of taillights through thick air. The yards'-high snowdrifts are north of us. This landscape's drama is of a smaller scale.

1903—President Roosevelt establishes Pelican
Island, Florida as first federal bird reserve

February 15   **TREEHOUSE**

 Crows are shuttling across the window corner where pine-needle draped and torn spider webs flap. These crows course the field beyond the

Sinking Creek Journal

pine row, but each passage miniaturizes them into visual toys of human perception. They talk in their extended families, and cruise human prognostication's flight lines. The leafless maple spreads between the crows and the human eye; even at 20° its every twig is bud-dotted, waiting for the gold that precedes the green. Nailed between its triple trunks are a crumpled treehouse's remains, collapsed carpeted beams. Each year following its abandonment it has risen higher inside its tree, until the trunk diversions unmoored it. The crow generations succeed each other, to the human eye always the same crows. Likewise the maple's growth would scarcely be noted if not for the treehouse's rises and falls, remembrances of times past.

2002—President Bush approves Yucca Mountain, Nevada, as nuclear waste disposal site

February 16   **CORPSE**

Ground crunches like shredded wheat, even beneath paws. All the streams are running, in bitter denial of this unremitting cold. Once or twice the spare rising sun kisses faces, then recedes. Only one corpse remains from warm growth—the clump of indian pipes, brown and flattened now, but in their prime rising scaled tubes bowed beside the trail. More like cicada husks in their death, they tangle, full and empty. This same colony has been here, like the crow family, forever. Watch and wait for its new May growth.

2005—Kyoto Protocol officially goes into force without U.S. acceptance

February 17   **STONE REMOVAL RULES**

It's said stone is being removed from the Cumberland Trail National Park, forty tons a day, by entities claiming mineral rights under sections of the park. A judge bans removal—stones aren't "minerals." Parts of the trail have collapsed as result of this removal. Stone is gold now—at least two ornamental shaleries in our city. It is sold by type—to builders and luxury homeowners for "natural look" landscaping. The irony needn't be belabored—park dismantled to become walkways and patio flooring in gated communities all over the Southeast. We, in our humble dwelling, are more fortunate than both—raised beds and patios, all born from Sinking Creek, mother of shapes and textures. Even here there are rules: no stone taken, however desirable, that is necessary to the streambank's integrity. All snails returned to the water. And the flat hillside shale blocks, propelled slowly downward year after year, are left to lie if they roof the dwelling of some nonhuman family.

1959—Vanguard 2, first weather satellite, launched

February 18　　　　　**WHITE VIBRATIONS**

It began to fall yesterday afternoon—single breath-melted flakes, thickening while the light went out, trees' branches dissolved into orbs of blue. The cat's yellow eyes upward, asking what are these little things, the collies crusted over, melting slowly, they look like a new breed. Wake to the white vibrations, clumps of flakes thrown from the pines, black squalling cloud clumps cross clearing skies—blinding housetop flash, then grey frontier, the greeting card-inal picturesque pose, strewn pepper thistle seeds and briefly permanent visible paw and foot track rhythm. A flash of memory—the lake effect snows of yesteryear—here, though, only a few inches, this time, this place.

1929—Migratory Bird Conservation Act passed

February 19　　　　　**HOME**

Look back, see home lights orange in the blue of gathering dawn. White sky eastward, road snaked black, collies scuff the snow. What do you feel about your home, a lightning bug in the beak of darkness, flame within a cold cave? Does it possess a permanence in your heart, can you claim its permanence though built by other hands on porous ground, subject to fire, wind, flood, electric failure? Though a glowing anomaly, a microspeck amid the homeless billions of the Earth? Reflect, while sky

Sinking Creek Journal

lightens in the east and the first bird stir shifts snowy pinetufts, whether your home is a true reality or but the false glow of a necessary illusion . . .

> " . . . a neuroscientist observed that despite all the cities in which he and his wife have lived, they always consider San Francisco to be 'home' . . . The magic they continue to feel when they visit . . .comes from the way their favorite haunts stir up their senses, unlocking a treasure chest of memories and feelings. . .the smell of crayons, the way sunlight falls on a staircase, the sound of rain pattering on the foliage of a certain kind of tree."
> Winifred Gallagher, **The Power of Place** (1993)

February 20   **LOST DUCKS**

These are the NGD—non-governmental ducks—exiles from the VA hospital's luxury pond, like unadmitted Vietnam vets gathering at the gates. Brush Creek bulges here, emerging from beneath Church Brothers, along Love Street, dead-rusted factories, abandoned residences occasionally burned for practice by the fire department. Other side: railroad spur, 4-lane, sign seemingly addressed to literate dogs: STAY ON LEASH. Don't Chase the Ducks. These ducks *are* frightened—mostly mallards, white hybrids, one black duck—they do not approach the human for bread, but herd away, down or upstream, between snags. The Lost Ducks, the ducks hugging the border between decadence and technology, ghost ducks of the unwild.

> "I have the sense that I am suspended in the middle of the lake with pelicans, coots, and grebes. I keep driving with the illusion that my old Peugeot station wagon is really a boat. When the lake starts seeping into the floorboards, I come to my senses. I stop the car, carefully open the door and climb on to the roof." Terry Tempest Williams, **Refuge** (1991)

February 21   **GREENING**

Deep night cloudburst, February thaw, all mud, scuffing uphill, sliding back: tiretracks mudwater full, the collies cavort. Trunks rain-stained, every winter green in the woods enlivened, intensified overnight. Boulders, rock outcrops green, feruled lichens erect. Twigpoints thrust forth. Surely there are cold nights ahead, but the vegetation seems to have both relaxed and turgidified at the molecular level, anticipation rooted in its bioplasm no less than in the human mind.

> "I <u>hear</u> not a sound, but I suddenly <u>feel</u> something enormous rolling through the world, shifting from the west into the east. A change in atmospheric pressure The forest grows still, expectant." Ken Carey, **Flat Rock Journal** (1994)

February 22   **AGAINST THE GRAIN**

The recent rain has run a sheet of water across Sinking Creek Road, gouging, as usual, the driveway. The landscape rectifiers did come, channelled and culverted it. Now an aluminum pipe, ugly, sticks out over the stream. But the rectifiers could not demolish and reforest the built environment; the homeless rainfall still flows, collecting leaves, debris, branches; the channel is clogged, the pipe is dry, the freed waters spread. This is a matter of gravity only in the literal sense, but it is a microcosm of the systemic distortion humans create when they build against the grain.

> 1972—EPA requires all gas stations to provide unleaded gas

February 23   **TRAIL OF BLOOD**

Tracking blood through the forest is easy. Every few feet leaves are shellacked as with exterior paint. Although they would be less visible in growing season, these little red pools make one realize how much jeopardy any wound creates in a balanced predator environment—and particularly to a domestic animal, like the border collie, whatever its agility. The trail of blood is an olfactory neon strip leading to pleasure and the kill. In this case it comes from one of the three nonchalant dogs—but which one? When each forays off the path, see if the drops continue. Turns out wherever Faye goes, the blood follows. She limps along gaily, pausing occasionally as usual to be sure the Master follows. For her, a cut pad, a lick, a wag. No problem.

Sinking Creek Journal

1977—Supreme Court says the EPA can issue blanket standards to control the industrial discharge of pollutants

February 24   **TWO CULTURES**

They ran a road along the ridge and called it, without irony, "Strawberry Fields." The houses live terraced over Sinking Creek valley, and the eye can follow the creek at a spyful distance, prying from above even into your own back yard. Now even more vertical barren hemlock tangles are for sale, and astride a dip there's a new "genuine log" house plastered with for sale signs. There are two sociogeostrata here, a worldwide motif, for the ridge houses sport foo dogs, carriageways and chandeliers, the valley ones porches, broken rockers, power boats on blocks, Jeff Gordon pennants. It's not clear that any cultural erosion has occurred; most of the ridge slope remains a scrappy wilderness, and maybe—who knows—a few old stills still hide out there.

1839—William Otis patents the steam shovel

February 25   **MUSCULAR ROOTS**

A quick thrash of rain, a front flashes through, by afternoon the sky is almost cloudless, then comes big wind, sun smiles at trees in torment. Out tossing balls, we all gaze at the old pinerow whipping around and wonder if any members will sever, plunge, impale, as happened once last year. The muscularity of these root systems impresses, though this is not Kansas, no John Muir swinging on sequoias, yet all the barren vegetation even here in this narrow valley vibrates, does not fall: every encounter of air temperatures, where'er it be, a new frontier of survival.

1885—fencing of public lands in the West prohibited by Congress

February 26   **WEED**

The bindweed so scrupulously derooted during January's thaw has managed covertly to regrow. Sunshine on the shoulder through shifting clouds and already the weeds in barren raised beds are alive. It is an honor to be weed. Pre-agraria, there are no weeds. Weed is often fruitful plant in wrong place at wrong time. Probably in neolithic forest clearing tree is clearing weed. Weed's condition is existential—not defined by essential nature but by figuration in human economy, particular place, particular time. Online popup ad is weed.

1972—Buffalo Creek flood in West Virginia kills 118

February 27   **ENFORCED RETIREES**

Now Faye's torn pad has become a sterile wrap from foot to knee. Needs to be dry, so plastic baggies and rubber bands go on if she needs the outdoors. She runs as a tripod. But border collies' domesticated sensitivity to their humans' rules is unparalleled. When Faye makes for the door, leg unprotected, Branna knows it, growls her down and belly-up. On many lists, border collies are the "most intelligent" breed. Their frustration manifests this intelligence—nothing to herd, no profession, in cold barren winter no Master's outdoor labor to monitor, they become restive as young retirees, cursing in their inner dogways the season and the Master. But they will persevere, if only as border guards, until spring comes, barking their way to meaningfulness.

> "In a dream within a dream I dreamt
> of all the animals crying out
> in their hidden places
> in the still silent places left to them . . ."
> Lawrence Ferlinghetti, "Rough Notes for a
> Rough Song of Animals Dying" (1978)

February 28   **BRANCHSITES**

Warm—the first wine-gnats in many a week. Though the sky begins to fishscale over, sun's been positively hot, flies buzz among the butterfly bush's dead blooms. You can see worm tracks patterning underwater leaves in the bog garden. Something's afoot. Tulip tops show, biding their time.

Sinking Creek Journal

Indefatigable dusty miller, parsley flaunt survival. New fennel fronds start rising through bones of the old. Green wild onion torches spot the lawn. Two cats and three dogs lie among all this, looking as though they know something. Cardinal performs its territorial. Out here, under the cucumber tree, you can look straight up at those fishscale clouds, their complex pattern, through a complex pattern of subdividing branches. Complex websites are built on this organic model of sequential subordination, but it's nicer to watch the branches and the clouds—Holy cow! February 28 and orange croci!

*1892—U.S. prohibition of fur seal hunting in
Bering Sea committed to arbitration*

March 1   **RACCOON**

Red sky at morning—splashed all over behind the mountains . . . dog rush to the creekbank . . . purposeful . . . animal alert . . . then again, a cry to the other side . . . all three rush against the fence . . . pine woodpile in the way. What's in the woodpile? Collies dance, try to approach some invisible entity, as usual the ferocious barking and white plume tails awag. Then their object comes into view: raccoon, massive as a meatloaf—but it's on the other side of the fence, seems to be trying to get to the dogs. Visions of rabies dance through the head . . . But again, raccoon is a usual suspect, treed at bird feeders before, maybe just prestorm confusion: torrents arrive and drumming windroar, shattered woodshards, all day, the trees hold on, into the evening, humans come and go, exclaiming, wheels grind gutters in mud . . . The roseate sky seems farther in the past than it is.

1872—Yellowstone National Park Act: first U.S. national park

March 2,
Baton Rouge, LA   **MISSISSIPPI**

Appalachia it ain't. Clover in the green slope to the levee, robins, mockingbirds, gulls on a mission. River anciently channelled here, upstream of disaster, imaging early spring order. Barges, linear, flat isobars, a steady north wind, subtle sun; you forget the scrub shore, surrounded

Fred Waage

by touristic artifacts, somewhat desultory Saturday noon—manicured yet abandoned. The old spaniolated state capitol, the USS Kidd with a little pirate flag; the levee stepped as though thousands of spectators might come simply to spectate the river and its commerce flow. GREATER BATON ROUGE MUNICIPAL PORT. A metallic ramp spirals from nowhere into the brown flow. 3 boyz on a rock, shadow snags under it. It is hard even to speak of the river, piercing our minds, our history, a doomsword of liquid light, murky undertow of fate . . .

1899—Mount Ranier National Park established

March 3
Baton Rouge, LA   **HISTORICAL DECONSTRUCTION**

Savannah it ain't. The built environment lost. Punched brass doors of Baton Rouge's "first skyscraper, 1913," National Registry of Historic Places, faded, barricaded. Empty Third Street, the historical plaques themselves decay. No restoration here. That which exists has always existed: Frosty's, America's Original Diner 1952, St. Joseph's Catholic church, skateboarding the *parvis*. Farmer's market on hot cement, all pottery, jewelry, Mardi Gras rejects, is closing up at noon. How slow was this disaster, lazy depopulation. Live oaks flourish sprawlingly on the courthouse lawn, surrounded by parking lots. The ironwork here is tentative, the long balconied brick commercial buildings are empty or inhabited only by lawyers. An allegorical fountain figure holds a sextant to commemorate all the Italian (immigrants?) who made Baton Rouge what it is today. What is it? Amethyst necklace with fleur-de-lys, $35 plus tax.

1849—United States Department of the Interior established

March 4   **CLEARANCE**

Baton Rouge it ain't. The Appalachian peaks are snowed, flakes fall through the chill below. The Gray area north of our city is a grey area indeed. There's a branch bank in every cleared cornfield. Tractor-roller aerates acreage beside ATM aerating money. Around here you'll find countless

Sinking Creek Journal

family gravesites, fenced, sometimes only two or three stones—at the highest point of a sloping field or pasture. If their dead converse, how do they talk about the malls stripping up toward them? Gray Station once was exactly that—a station on the line—a quarter century ago the only businesses here were a Dairy Queen at the corner of Suncrest and Gray Station Road, and the Appalachian Fairgrounds. Now it hums with formless sleekness. The DQ is still there, epicenter, archaic as the old Baton Rouge courthouse.

1912—first U.S. law regulating the shooting of migratory birds passed

March 5   **ECOTONE**

Crows mate atop a telephone pole . . . yellow llamas mill in a condo-ringed farmyard. Out here almost all the unbuilt acreage is Available. Just west of where the Bentley family cemetery overlooks Kohl's and Lowe's, on the left the Knob Creek Church of the Brethren asserts a past: puritanically white and clear, short-steepled, ancient thick-boled maples. Congregation formed 1799, oldest in Tennessee. This church is 102 years old. Take narrow Fairview Road just beyond it and you are within an ecotone: to the left the gouged read ends of the no longer Available acreage, flattened and terraced for "med/tech" space; to the right, agraria, cattle crazing in short grass greener than February, slurping, a wandery watercress streamlet. There's a former farm pond, green, deoxygenated, and bulldozers' tipple, house high boulders wildly tumbled, the old one lane cement-arched, trash-lined railroad underpass. Honk and pray. Emerge, fractured houses and the bulldozer-gashed land receding, as you go deeper, each tumbledown trailer like a breath of fresh air.

1970—Nuclear Nonproliferation Treaty goes into effect

March 6   **STONE MEMORIES**

Slowly warming every day here, warm enough to clear the raised beds. As they've evolved, freestone circles a couple of feet high, through population explosion married into ovals. All the stones have been hauled from Sinking Creek over the years; anthropocentrism: the Chosen Stones.

Stones interlock in infinite possible combinations, winter-tumbled ones may end up in new beds. They're lifted for the thread-fine weed roots to be unniched, or the ingenious cramped false strawberry to be unrooted. Dead sunflower stalks, beebalm, butterfly weed, levelled. Some would have done this in the fall, but it is a sentimental indulgence to imagine the old cycle grazing the new. And to the human cultivator, the memory of one season's flowers, insects, spiderwebs, snaps out with each culled stalk.

"Stone gathering became a real preoccupation on our walks or drives, and it was a rare day when we did not come back 'with stone in hand.'" Helen and Scott Nearing, **Living the Good Life** (1954)

March 7   **THE VULTURES KNOW**

Out to a flapping of vultures. They're back! They rise and maneuver through bare branches, resettle, gaze down to the collies in translated contempt. What does their residency mean? Perhaps there is new activity—and mortality—among the small mammals as air warms. Picking wind-downed branches, trying to imagine what vultures may perceive in the cold grass. Maybe they're here purely for r & r. They weigh heavily in the mind, strange fruit in a fruitless wood. The vultures know something, though. Wind is rising, daffodils bloom across the road, the cardinal couple sit on front porch rail, eyeing the cardinal-red front door with a strange nesting look, as though they have fledglings in their eyes.

"Now there are seven of them, in little tall black circles
    'Look, Darl,' I say; 'see?'
He looks up. We watch them in little tall black circle of not-moving
    'Yesterday there were just four,' I say."
                William Faulkner, **As I Lay Dying** (1930)

March 8   **PRUNING THOUGHTS**

How the air has warmed since yesterday! High garden preparation mode. Moving and removing stones, beetles and ground spiders scurry. Even the earthworms seem more prolific. The daylillies lining the yard

Sinking Creek Journal

have sprouted. The boxelder buds. The baby beebalm leaves, so intrusive, fill all their bed's surface, need to be surgically removed from the sedum. A thought of this anthropoid urge to prune and clear: mere flowerbeds though they be, is there any qualitative difference between it and the urge to build, say, a new shopping mall? Can the gardener without hypocrisy condemn the developer? Is the urge even that exclusively humanoid? When cat Ki rotates on the quilt to press down the virtual grass, has he not intruded his own space into the fabric grassland? You can prune and clear your mind of thought by clambering down, sitting streamside, imagining joy in the splashing streamfall over stones. Young longtailed salamanders, brown backs, black sides, scuttle to safety. Leif lets his tennis ball roll down the slope, waits above, ready to sprint. Ready to sprint is this day.

> "It feels savage to chop off healthy plants just when they're surging up thick and green. The euphemism we use is 'cutting back,' when what we mean is <u>cut them off at the knees!</u>" Diane Ackerman, **Cultivating Delight: A Natural History of My Garden** (2001)

March 9   **MULCHING**

Hauling and spreading compost, mulch. Sweat is on. Cleared, the gardens look barren, the earth dry. All the cosseted speak their deprivation. For some, it is too late—the magnificent globe rosemary could not survive below 10°. Still fragrant, it totters on its dead stem. Sterile nutrients in plastic bags! Our ancestors used their own night soil and still the species survives. A critical crow caws its screed from the cucumber tree. The beds are all tucked in, one by one, careful not to cover new as yet anonymous shoots. The woodshards and soil smell strong, spill out as though released from an unnatural confinement . . . into a more natural one.

1975—work begins on the Alaska Pipeline

March 10   **PLANT TERRORIST**

The Delta of Dogs it has been called, wooded flat triangle where the property's streams and seepages converge. It is not yet impenetrable, as it will be. One can look across it and the Nameless Stream, at the trout lily mottled leaves in ranks, turgid, not yet flowering. Here, stone cliff across the way, all alone at stream edge, a plant like a vision, wooded stem, opposed, thin, sharply pinnate irregular ovoid leaves. Defiantly green, it peaks to greenish-white clusters, plump, clumped, hanging, half-fruit, half-flower. *Mahonia aquifolium*, Oregon Grape, related to barberries, invasive species. From whence could it have invaded, creating its own midwood solitude? It looks frighteningly confident, centered, like a terrorist in your house.

*1957—Dalles Dam (Columbia River) floodgates
close, inundating Native American fisheries*

March 11   **COMPANION INVADERS**

Outthrust rock strata, steep rise, east of Sinking Creek, limestone, sandstone, each table separate, form walkways, animal tread clears them, hardwood and juniper for human handholds, synclinous, spypoint to back yards directly below. Each outcrop provides shallow, deep, dry shelter, reaching far back. Somewhere deep here copperheads wait the coming of heat. Somewhere along these floating ridges there is a deep vertical shaft. It is suddenly encountered—two feet wide, depthless. You could fall in. Found long ago, and lost. Another expedition, another failure. Only the collies are happy. Long ago when children were little there was a nest lodged part-way down the shaft, and in the nest a single blue egg. Where is it now in this jungle of parallels? Trekking back, a brown snail shell whorled upwards—very pretty to display—whoa! This is a live snail, going our way, only more slowly, *viviparus georgianus*, another invasive species, well established, coursing the limestone with two other invasive species, one quadripedal, one biped.

1824—Bureau of Indian Affairs created in the War Department

March 12   **FIRST RED**

Nature's first green is red, it seems. The eccentric red maple that creates the shade garden has suddenly sprung red flowerets at each twig

Sinking Creek Journal

tip. Insects swarm them. These are not flowers, of course—they are the first baby branching leaves and will soon fall to green. Another overnight birth is of the trout lily flowers, so soon to bloom, so soon to fade. They cluster above the cave while shakeaway woodchuck repellent ("totally organic") is spread, and even the curious collies turn away in disgust. Trout lillies' lance-shaped yellow petals rakishly curl back, tawny anthers in meticulous contrast. Today is bog garden spring cleaning—heavy sodden leaves and mud lifted up to dike the further bank. Water flow is too slow, watercress starting out must be ruthlessly cleared. Moving down muddy channel, leveed over many years, the first crawfish, scrabbling desperately, dives hard . . .

1888—"*Blizzard of '88*" *kills 400*

March 13   **NEWNESS IS AFOOT**

Cats can tell the fauna are rising to sun, sun occluded only by horsetail clouds. Cats stalk with range and purpose through grass imperceptibly thickening. Yesterday Ki had a bird (species unknown) struggling in his mouth. Ki, an aging cat, defiant. Ultimately Branna relieved him of this burden. Newness is afoot. First butterfly—a mourning cloak, sleek black wings rimmed white, a hot fudge sundae. First wasp. Pair of broad-winged hawks chasing each other, among the stream trees, mew felinely in flight. And the nuthatch! Years ago a beautiful backyard maple suffered Sudden Tree Death Syndrome. Decay and dangerous rope demolition have reduced it to a raddled forty-foot stub, a harvest log for insect eaters. The nuthatch has created or discovered a perfect nest hole just below the stub's top. It looks down upon wretched humans on their deck, skips pridefully in and out the hole, upside down, head cocked, listening for applause.

1991—*Exxon agrees to pay 1 billion to clean up Exxon Valdez oil spill*

March 14   **BORING BEES**

"Room-temperature" outdoors in mid-March, mechanical noises aborning. Lots of firsts today with clear 70°. First mosquito arrives on the arm. Not the tiny highspeed dark Japanese variety of late summer, but a dignified mosquito with a black line down its back and grey on each side. It deserves an award. Then the carpenter bees, emerging from hibernation, cruising the wood-walled apartment, the toolshed, for a good place to drill. Eastern carpenter bees (we've called them boring bees, and they do get boring after awhile), *xylocopia virginia*, are big, black, and fuzzy. They look like bumblebees without the yellow and without the sting. They drill straight round holes for homes in any available wood surface. High spring you can stand under the walls and their sawdust snows on you. Boring bees have strong personalities—when they claim a space, they don't like to be disturbed. They'll hover before a human, stare straight in the eyes. It is useless to persecute boring bees; after they've completed their holes they become discreet, very content it seems in the semi-domestic ecosystem.

1988—U.S. Senate ratifies ozone layer protection treaty

March 15 **PEAR PRESSURE**

Cultivars are also beginning their short careers of ostentation—the neighbors' Bradford Pear tree, for example. The Bradford Pear seems to be the favorite ornamental tree of the Upper South. Its symmetry and white petals seem to reflect a mood of domestic stability and prosperity. To the radical, its ubiquity become irritating. It's a Stepford tree. It grows under false pretences—it's actually from China, *pyrus calleryana*, brought over in the early 20th century to be the "perfect street tree." Despite being raised near good homes, in some areas it goes wild, takes over, loses its shape, becomes thorny. Like many pretty things, it smells bad—it has been said its flowers' scent could be compared with decaying seafood, dog vomit, dried urine, human semen. Who was Bradford, anyway?

"*Invaders now make up one-fifth to one-third of all North American plant species, and their share of territory is even greater.*" Evan Eisenberg, **The Ecology of Eden** *(1998)*

March 16   **FORSYTHIA**

Steady, even rain falls on the unlatching forsythia blossoms, straggled along their unkempt hedge. They are fully blown in less shaded areas. These blooms have not yet recovered from being pruned at the wrong time. Unlike the Bradford pear, the forsythia appears to be a favored adoptee all over the habitable U.S. Its lyrical name disguises its anthropocentric origin, William Forsyth, eighteenth-century botanist. Like so many Western decoratives it was introduced from the Eastern hemisphere, and has been intensely hybridized. As hedging, it is yin to the Bradford Pear's yang, and as prodigious outreaching imperialist must be continually pruned. Those little yellow flowers streaming along the branches flourish for so short a time—the taking in of a breath—it is fortunate the leaves are so richly green. Ours seek all summer to invade the yard, must be kept in their place, but are otherwise left to enlace, enwrap, and do their thing. They cover a continent of trash and make an essential fringe of wildness to host winged and scurrying creatures.

1978—Amoco Cadiz oil spill, Portsall Rocks off Brittany

March 17   **FRIGHT IN THE NIGHT**

Snowflakes pour from the sun, they disgorge in flocks, like the veering birds. They settle and glaze new-sprung leaf edges. Sinking Creek has swollen for the first time in many months, its rock shoals revealed only by patterns of disturbance, back-eddies. Condensed to a narrows, it hurtles the bend beneath bedroom windows, a steady low roar like that of the appliances the rivers it flows into power. Later, there's a fright in the night. Tam Lin the cat flees his isolation ward in deep chill and freezing rain, we call his name, slash through briars, stream, up muddy slope. Woodchuck cave is empty, we're wailing; what will the neighbors think? "If we leave the windows open maybe he'll come back." *Mon Dieu!* We struggle in, and there he sits in the middle of the dining table, embandaged. "Where y'all been?"

1978—U.S. bans CFC's (chlorinated fluorocarbons)

March 18   **COLD**

Finally Faye's pawpad is healed enough for her to go up the mountain. Now it's cold again, the terrain all returned to winter state, ice crystals, bare branches, frail firs fallen over. All that's evidently changed are the trout lily flowers, closed now into reddish spires. This morning it seems the chill will never end. The woods have paused in their unfolding, wait the great warmup predicted for days ahead. Winter is almost over chronologically, but here, in these mountains, it seems it will *de facto* never end.

1925—worst tornado in U.S. history kills 689 in Indiana

March 19   **STONESCAPE**

Chill morning has mellowed to cloudy warmth. Up the trail to spread more fox urine around the woodchuck cave. Trout lilies open again, more than ever. Cut the barbed wire artifacts of earlier regimes. We all tumble down streamward, a hail of leaves. Feel the rock moss, curled, upstanding, springy, stonecrops threading and spreading their ruddy heads among it. There are all sorts of angled outthrust surfaces around the woodchuck cave. The board hauled down doesn't begin to cover this gaping geometer's dream. One humped white stone juts out of the Nameless Stream's sand below, ganglia root down into it. Higher up, secret rock cleft, hepatica row bows thin stems, even more ephemeral than the lilies. Hard and gentle fused in this stonescape.

"Their nemesis this spring was porcupines in the strawberry patch. Their solution at first was simply to trap the spiny creatures and remove them, but for the past week . . . the porcupines had been winning the battle. Bev had set up a watch the night before to confront the animals, stationing herself between the rows with a firewood-splitting ax in hand. She hadn't been there long when a porcupine waddled out of the woods . . . 'Then it nosed right into a strawberry bush and started eating! I raised the ax to whack it, but . . . oh, what's a few strawberries?'"
Jack Nisbet, **Purple Flat Top: In Pursuit of a Place** (1996)

Sinking Creek Journal

March 20   **WILLOW**

    Willow is the first to utter leaves. Already today the new ones cascade gracefully, but not in the alien weeping willow's stylized symmetry. Ours is the black willow, *salix nigra*, complex and asymmetrical black trunk and branches. There's one just up the road, cramped between tarvia and creek. The powerline liberators have spared it. There's "our" willow at the creekbend, grown under the great elm's shelter until the disease hit. Across the bog garden there's a new young willow, overshaded—needs more light—one pole of a half-failed elliptical "blue garden." At the other pole, and ornamental untreestanding braided willow acquired at some arbor day treefest. It seemed too delicate for this world, but still breaks forth. You can see the yellow catkins hanging from each black willow bract, waiting for pollinators. The mourning cloak spotted a few days ago may have overwintered in a cranny of our black willow, may fertilize its flowers, may deposit eggs on its bark; its caterpillars may eat the willow's leaves, pupate from its branches, spread their wings in its care.

1954—William O. Douglas and other environmentalists walk the C & O Canal

March 21   **IMPENDING GREEN**

    Acrid incinerated garbage scent borne on misty, humid air, carries sounds far. The garbage truck grinding lifts our offal out of sight, carries it to the brimming landfill that exudes methane. Today fire siren and coalcar rumble seem very near, even high in the woods. Sun rises like a headlamp over Buffalo Mountain. Birdsong fills the woods—three pileated woodpeckers chase and call, then do their vertical curl to land on neighboring trunks. Recent rains have drawn down much bark, twigs, ruffle-lichened branches; one long stripped treetrunk, the fresh hollow its clubbed white-fungused root left is so shallow it's a wonder it did not fall sooner. The groundpine colonies seem to have spread, the fern and feather moss overreaching, a whole new colony of starry white hepatica among the dump's rusty chair limbs and mouldy white dishdrainers. Droplets condense beside budlets. A sense of impending green.

First Earth Day—1970

March 22   **SPIKY RISINGS**

Season of spiky risings. In the 70s and growth-odor, fresh, non-point source fragrance. Beds of green nails. Weaving them, Faye tosses a dead chipmunk at the ideal stage—rigor mortis but not rotten. Bored, then she turns the same attention on her stuffed hedgehog. Surely the chipmunk has a more appealing fragrance. Apparently she can choose to ignore the difference for the purpose of kinetic pleasure. Is this creative imagination? Scattered at the edges of the dump, among pine saplings, one finds shattered needle-clumps from plastic Christmas trees. There's congruence here. The life of artifice—is it really any less a life? For canine and human, the art itself is nature.

United Nations World Day for Water

March 23   **MAYAPPLES**

Ridgetop, the whole ravaged farmstead bare below: cattle, green pasture the other side, a silver stream sparkling into a farm pond. Here the same tattered uprooted tree piles, firebronzed, charcoaled treadridges, the mercy trees ringed with red ribbons. The collies dash about this wasteland—but wait—there is new growth. The scraping wasn't deep enough to take all the bulb-plants, so amid the barrens are patches of daffodils, both blown and in leaf, careless as when they by Windermere bloomed, conveying in imagination that pseudo-stable rurality. Reluctantly back in the present, downhill, woods again, the hepatica again, stars in the dump, and accidental leaf-scuff and a leap into the future, rising, still tightly coiled green nubs, the first of next month's mayapples, *podephyllum peltatum*, which will unfurl umbrella leaves, white flowers, berries. For weeks these poisonous umbrellas will enshade this ruptured landscape of dead mattresses and broken wheelchairs, presences so vivid everything else becomes backdrop.

1889—Benjamin Harrison opens Oklahoma
Territory to white settlement as of April 22

Sinking Creek Journal

March 24   **Territory**

Heat snap here—all over the Southeast, premature budding everywhere, everything is being rushed into bloom like kids on the college prep track, even our snowball bush, which didn't use to bloom until May. A blue skipper dancing, yellow wasps preening and exploring house orifices for nest sites. Birds territorialize, creating exclusive three-dimensional homesteads, neighboring airholdings imperceptible to human senses. Bradford pear blooms fading to leaf already. Tam Lin has been biopsied, diagnosed with an autoimmune affliction, somehow triggered by the woodchuck attack. We've decided he can't live his life in a darkened room, despite the angry red patches on his neck and face. Let him be a cat among cats, even if he dies being one. Before he's sprung, the woodchuck cave is catproofed—old boards, fence posts, plastic mesh, even—god forbid—styrofoam. The barricader tries to think like a cat and countless ingresses reveal themselves. Every chink is a fatal possibility. But liberated now, Tammy wags his tail-stump, claws a log. He's Back.

1989—Exxon Valdez incident, Prince William Sound

March 25   **Empty Pond**

It may peak today—steaming up. Sumac fans unfurl, mayapple hands begin to reach out, spiderwebs band the passing brow. Millipedes uncurl amid the leaves—big flat ones, black with violent yellow spots; smaller ones with scarlet-banded backs. The sweaty destination is an empty earth-walled pond, niched in a woodslope, hemlocks surround it. Damp now, a visit to a memory. In 1980 this was a cattle pond at the southwest corner of the Bastian farmstead, muddy water for the bovids still wandering the woods to drink, immerse in; perfect for turning a border collie all black. There was for the pond a time of change like Spring—afforestation would make the habitat untenable for cows; the dark water would endure only to lose its source eventually and evaporate. Now we stand in a sort of agrarian tomb, while all around the tall growth buds.

Fred Waage

> *"Years ago, when the land beyond the brook was pasture, this was someone's retreat. We can imagine some winsome dairy mild dangling her bare feet in the dappled waters, and perhaps of a rare June evening the squire himself would break off from his interminable labors, come to this spot, and admire his stonework, the wooded bank across the stream, and the last songs of the wood thrush."* John Hanson Mitchell, **Walking Towards Walden** (1995)

March 26 — TILLERS

Tractors have begun their pilgrimages up and down Sinking Creek Road, answering the call to plow garden plots. The tractor engines have a distinctive, percussive aural redolence and their drivers always seem to be old males in overalls and straw hats, as though they've ridden up, grizzled Demeters, from half a century ago to freshen the present's earth. Of course, like second growth they are not originals. They are interstitial: when the valley was first cleared and planted, everyone was a cultivator, everyone cultivated h/her own. Big farms died, properties shrank, houses moved closer together, but still there remained land to till. The time will come for sure when the valley will be close-packed and the largest tiller will be a Mantis.

> *"No one dreamed, a hundred years ago, that metal, air, petroleum, and electricity could coordinate as an engine. Few realize today that soil, water, and animals are an engine, subject, like any other, to derangement. Our present skill in the care of mechanical engines did not arise from fear lest they fail to do their work. Rather was it born of curiosity and pride of understanding. Prudence never kindled a fire in the human mind; I have no hope for conservation born of fear."* Aldo Leopold, "The Farmer as Conservationist" (1939)

March 27 — HYACINTHS

Grape hyacinths under the old snowball bush, almost the first bulbs planted here; marginalized, they still return, maybe not even noticed some years except when the bush is cut back. So much inhabitance history, stories of day and night, years gone by implied in these organic emblems of return. Humans imagining futures as they were planted, those futures now pasts, inconceivable then, no less inconceivable now when they bloom the same again.

1851—First reported white sighting of Yosemite

March 28 **BLUE SEASON**

All seems blue now—bushy lyre-leafed sage opening, everywhere violets, purple or purple and white, spotting cultivated spaces with cute abandon, as though proclaiming a plant's universal right to volunteer. Grey vultures fill the sycamores, dark on light, swivel their leatherheads, flap heavily to new branches. One perches on the rock right above the woodchuck cave. Soon they will be tilting in the wind. Floral time moves fast: few trout lily flowers remain, and incongruous dandelions strive through rock cracks. How did their delicate down drift there? The comfrey is rising, a patch of oval leaves, eventually a spike displaying blue flowers.

1979—Three Mile Island meltdown

March 29 **BUCKEYE AND FIDDLEHEAD**

Chiller morning. Faye's shrill cries trail the white tails that flash uphill between trees. Fiddlehead colonies rising from fern centers, curled like fiddles' scrolls, green softened with brownish down, prelude to new fronds; fiddleheads widely edible and sometimes poisonous, symbols of a new stage in Spring's uncurling. Part of a trinity—ramps, morels, fiddleheads—that have come to express the Appalachian culture that prizes and displays its connection to them. Unlike ginseng, whose endangerment has internationalized its identity, these three remain at home. Another species, differently unfurling now on these rocky slopes is the Ohio State Tree, the buckeye, each branch of which ends in a five-finger palmate hand, slowly opening now. In autumn, plenty of its nuts (which, to Native Americans, resembled bucks' eyes) provide mast all along the slopes. It is an ambitious species, right now the understory is filled with three to four foot saplings, greenly optimistic, mingling with the redbuds.

Fred Waage

> "The mixed mesophytic [forest] turns out to be a huge place . . . Almost as big as New England. And in the forest live some eighty species of trees. The forest canopy alone can consist of three dozen different tree species—basswoods, magnolias, some of them rare species, may kinds of oak and hickory, a 'forgotten' subspecies of locust, the nearly extinct red mulberry, and beech, maples, tulip poplar, buckey, sweetgum." Charles E. Little, **The Dying of the Trees** (1995)

March 30   **EFT**

There are forty-seven known species of salamanders in the Southern Appalachians, more than in any other temperate zone. Bounding up the rocks, the collie group tramples all around a blood-red juvenile Eastern Newt, *notophtalmus viridescens*, in its eft stage, right at the stairstep rocks' peak. Upright on its legs, in a posture of paralyzed fear, one imagines its humanized thought as "O my God! I'm done for!" The careless collies pass on, the newt is safe. Of the twenty-three threatened amphibians on the USFWS list, thirteen are salamanders. This solitary newt standing alone against a thoughtless onrush of mammals makes one think of the world beyond Sinking Creek and how many creatures out there are being crushed in the heedless rush of human endeavor.

1983—First California Condor chick born in captivity

March 31   **OLD MILL**

In every roadside ditch the yellow mustards are in bloom, as here by this culvert over Knob Creek. This road, once freely coursing the pastures, has been rudely amputated; shopping centers and superhighway cut it off. Black Angus cattle still graze by Knob Creek, and a Canada Goose tilts its head toward the Lowe's next door. Streamside trees are budded out. Further back is a log farmstead you can visit "by appointment only," and across the road, the original Denny's Mill, after which the road was named. The mill must, like the farmstead, date from the late eighteenth century, with its whitewashed stone foundation and massive square wood

Sinking Creek Journal

upper story. It has not fallen in on itself, but looks as though it soon will. A realtor's sign fronts it. Surrounded by the cheerful yellow mustards, it looks like an old Silenic, Falstaffian figure—awaiting—one last fling? Or death?

1933—Reforestation Unemployment Act initiates the CCC

April 1   FLOWERING TREES

This is a Great Leap Forward day for all flowering trees. Two days of rainshowers have quelled pine pollen, and freshness fills the air. Redbuds, tame and wild, flourish, as do as yet unblighted dogwoods. Purple phlox has clumped at the driveway entrance as though by design. The Japanese cherry, thrust in inhospitable earth twenty years ago, begins its fleeting rosy reign as false Janus to this postage stamp of native plantlife. The most extrusive phenomena are the pollynoses beginning to helicopter all over the yard, eager to give birth to maplets in every possible fertile corner, even crotches of other trees, but particularly in rich gutter humus. Until it is cleared, the guttering looks like the first step in a green roofing enterprise.

1970—Cigarette Ads on TV outlawed by
Public Health Cigarette Smoking Act

April 2   FIRST CUT

It's time for the first cut. Actually, past time, due to mechanical problems. Whatever the ecological status of lawnmowing, it allows the mower to taste anew the land's contours, survey the cultivated growth, observe the population changes in grasses and weeds from the year before. For example, wild mustard, yellow and sprawly, is dominant this year on the marginal spaces. Ragwort has volunteered again around the bog—bunches of miniaturized sunflower blooms on tall stalks. The apple blossoms are already in bud, white pear ones cascade down, mint marches into the grass, blue-eyed weeds creep toward garden plots, bare earth stripped by the paws of winter where so laboriously seeded the summer before. Scouting for upthrust bones, old slippers, doggy toys—so much history to clog the blades. And afterwards the newmown scent, the good fresh wounds, satisfaction of the level.

1819—First successful U.S. agricultural journal,
The American Farmer, *founded*

April 3   **MOONSET**

At 6 AM full moon is setting, gold in a ring of cream, orange rim, a cosmic *crème brulée*. The moon ring warns of a predicted dogwood winter: "If it thunders in January, it will snow in April," and there was thunder during our January heat wave. But snow seems far away this hot cloudless day, mockingbirds proclaiming Spring, twin red tulips flaunting their lips, new residents like the long-tailed Brown Thrasher scrabbling neighborly beside mourning doves, tigerlillies' new offspring bending fountain leaves, sky unearthly blue until the first drops begin to fall and ciphering crows pronounce a new dispensation.

"This is the moment, that moment which may last for a day or a week, depending on the wind and weather. It is the time when tree green trembles between wary bud and opening leaf, when a few hours of concentrated sunlight could almost change the face of the land." Hal Borland, **Sundial of the Seasons** *(1964)*

April 4   **FRANKLINIA**

Thunder in the night; grey day and chill. Northern Gods invade, as yet not full force. Time to overcoat the exposed with mulch, the unexpected resurrected Japanese painted fern in its wooden tub, the just-budding treasured Franklinia. This Franklinia was born and bought at Monticello itself. *Franklinia altamaha* grows slowly in the Appalachian elevations, and it may be many years—maybe not—before it gloriously blooms white with golden center. There's human pride in "owning" such a mythical individual. The Bartrams found a grove of them on Georgia's Altamaha River in 1765. William gathered seeds and named the species for Benjamin.

The grove and all its trees vanished, so all the living individuals descend from William's harvest. So scarce are they that your own Franklinia, like this one, can be registered on the tree's official website—but don't expect to get a *family* tree back in exchange: between 1998 and 2000 only 2,000 individuals were registered.

"The trees are, of course, larger and different than they were then, especially the ones close to the house that block out the sun's light. The majestic bald cypress is gone; the pond is dried up The Franklinia tree died, but was replaced, so it still lives. . . John Bartram's gardens are dead. Clues to their contents are buried under the ground, where fossilized pollen awaits a curious twenty-first-century archaeologist who wants to know more about plants." Thomas P. Slaughter, **The Natures of John and William Bartram (1996)**

April 5   **FALSE PERCEPTION**

The big chill has well and truly descended upon the upper South, and freeze warnings have been issued for the next two nights. That has not prevented the budding of the forest. Approaching our wooded slope, with Buffalo Mountain, its TV towers, its black patches of beetled dead pine trunks looming above, you can see a wall of light green tints, unnamable profligate tonalities, not filled in yet, pointillistic, full of promise. Already the rock faces are concealed. Hardwood dominance is clear from panoramic distance. Only when you enter the real depths do the gatherings of hemlock, cedar, white pine, appear. It is thus rich to consider the limits of environmental perception. How many "deep" physical environments does one actually physically enter? How much environmental perception consists only of deceptive panoramic distant eyeshots? How much detailed truth must the concerned human feel obliged to absorb? It seems doubtful that first-world human cultures could survive without willed false perception. Beneath our slope's tree cover may be a thousand stills, or "illicit distilleries." The best example of surface perception is fringe preservation beside roadways. Surrounded, as you think, by forest, you flash past a gap and behold!—all behind the fringe is a treeless, plantless, plain.

*1824—Audubon presents his work to the
Academy of Natural Scientists in Philadelphia*

April 6   **FREEZE**

A survey of the first night's freeze damage at morning, temperature 33°. As much new growth as damage. By the streamlet the first fleabanes —soon to spread everywhere—have bloomed, to complement the neighboring yellow ragwort with pinkish white stars. Down in Sinking Creek's rocky border plateau arrowheads have arisen, their arrow leaves distinct, not ready yet to bloom. Most pronounced are the first flowerings of dwarf crested iris, *iris cristata*, on the steepest west-facing slopes under Dead Man's Pass. The iris mingle, share space, with, and immediately supersede, the trout lilies, as comrades in roots. Though their flowers are tiny, they are delightfully complex, the petals displaying diverse tonalities of blue, and protruberant sepals. They seem to unfurl by the moment, untouched by cold. Further into the woods, leaves on hardwood saplings have crumpled, folded inward, while others, baby butternuts and hickories, expand tumescent. In places, the mayapple umbrellas are slightly furled, but the fiddleheads still curl up and the partial buds of later leaves still unfurled seem safely encased. Let us wait and see what tonight's deeper freeze will wreak.

"All my life I have been heading for the country, not to re-create a happy childhood, but to grant myself the gift of haws, the geography of flowing water." Philip Lee Williams, **Crossing Wildcat Ridge** *(1999)*

April 7   **APRIL SNOW**

As twilight fell, so did the snow, short sharp gusts amid the dogwood and cherry blossoms. The carnage overnight is clear this morning. Snowflakes pepper the deep green grass, coat stream slopes and leaf piles; airborne, a few still dance. So many already emerged plants are prostrated, leaf-fallen. The freeze-died tissue is dark, and appears swollen: Virginia bluebells, beebalm, columbine, even the sedum, whose leaves so sturdy and thick are now flopped over like collie ears. Are they gone or will they rise again? We didn't think we needed to cover the gardens, but were sadly mistaken. It's not only plants. It is said that wasps, their hibernatory "antifreeze" dissipated, will die *en masse*, and the summer plant predators they prey on will flourish. Indeed it is ironic that the day a definitive and dark international global warming report is released this microcosm has been crippled by cold.

> "She loved the look of it, light, powdery flakes that seemed to vanish as they floated gracefully to the ground. She loved the feel of it, the wet, cool shock as it touched the skin of her upturned face. She loved the way it seemed to displace sound. No airplane ever seemed so loud in the falling snow, no boat, truck, or snow machine. Falling snow toned a shout down to a murmur and then absorbed the murmur, imposing its own sweet, silent hush on a noisy world." Dana Stabenow, **A Fine and Bitter Snow** (2002)

April 8   **COLD AGAIN**

Cold Wave, day 3: it's not a fallen white petal, it's a frozen cabbage butterfly attached to a twig. The buckeyes' palms of green are collapsed, all five fingers fallen together like so many furled umbrellas. Sheila, the nursery manager, says all perennials regrow from the root; as long as the root doesn't freeze, they will recover. We noticed this yesterday, when the columbine's leaves stretched out again. Some plants do seem unaffected, for example false solomon's seal, yet to bloom, the curved stems' alternating ovate leaves are flat and unblemished. All those pink apple buds, blossoms, though, are rust-orange. Will this be the Year Without Apples?

> "If one pried up earth with a stick on those days, one found raised shafts of ice slender as needles and pure as spring water." Marilynne Robinson, **Housekeeping** (1981)

April 9   **LINKS**

No one's out on the golf course now except the disc-er. The fairways are all frosted. The sand grains must be ice-fused. Are the ghosts of golfers past out this morning? This rolling expanse of green grass and full-bodied trees was once a vibrant mixed-race working class community until it was Urban Renewed and its residents dispersed. Surely, you might say, this was, from an environmental viewpoint, an improvement. Consider this: if human communities are part of "nature," is their destruction or dispersal "against nature"? Is golf course not a monoculture that erases the biodiversity of weedplots, kitchen gardens, untended hedges, nourished by the offal of a hundred outhouses? If the green belt (links, park, footpath . . .) is a chastity belt, what fecundity is lost?

"The country club exemplified the trend in which suburbs moved later in the twentieth century, when almost an end in itself . . . as leisure time increased, compulsive play became an accepted alternative to compulsive work. Real nature was forgotten in the midst of manicured greens and all-weather tennis courts." Kenneth T. Jackson, **Crabgrass Frontier** *(1985)*

April 10   **CARNAGE**

    Red-tail hawk rises, flaps east; three crows head west, a vulture flies beneath jet trails. Omens are as usual ambiguous, but Authority says the three-day freeze is ending and the leaves will rise again. The apple orchardists of Unicoi County have lost a lot—the further advanced the bloom, the more fatal the freeze. This is strawberry time in East Tennessee. The strawberry farmers have coated their plants, at great cost, in ice, to keep them at 32°. On Sinking Creek one can observe mixed carnage. Dogwood whites hang limp and shrivelled. The most resilient, unfazed plant appears to be the common dandelion. It's dynamics at the cellular level: in the allium garden, every chive stalk has flopped over—the patch resembles a green punk hairdo—while all the garlic stalks still stand at attention. Fortunately the butterfly bushes have not bloomed yet—their leaves are crumpled. Even at ten AM though, the sun's rays already now pierce hotly to the surface of earth, boding a resurgence.

1872—J. Sterling Morton initiates first Arbor Day in Nebraska City

Sinking Creek Journal

April 11   **HERON PATIENCE**

From the bedroom window you can watch the great blue heron in Sinking Creek, scarcely twenty feet away, an unknowing intimate. Here it looks much smaller than in flight. It stands now at the cold stream edge, intent on whatever it seeks below the bubbling surface. What prey can there be? It is too early for minnows and many other heron foods like dragonflies and baby water snakes. It hardly needs such stalking behavior for somnolent snails. Now, with ineffable deliberation it slowly walks to the stream's center, its clawed feet enter the water without a riffle, it reaches the further shore. With no less deliberation it pivots, faces the way it came. Its stare seems to intensify, it opens its bill part way like a nutcracker, holds this pose. The human observer, though struck with admiration, wants action, but the heron's currency is patience and immobility. An impatient heron would starve. A few hours later it is gone—upstream, or downstream to the Holston. Its presence is a gift of brevity and silence.

1964—Agricultural Act of 1964 providing soil conservation acreage signed by President Johnson

April 12   **SPRING STREAM**

For what was the great blue heron setting its beak? The clumsy human feet have no standing where complex stony fjords, minuscule waterfalls and standing pools yield beneath flat force. The human tread is like the trunkated (sic.) metal stake, fused to a chunk of concrete, lodged among stream-smoothed stones. But then again the sculpturing flow has arranged the human artifact in a space of almost unnoticeable repose, it has found an antitype kinship. In any case the chill sundrenched Spring stream refreshes—purple phlox across the way, snail-spotted stones and shifting shadow, spattering as uneven waters pass beneath new leaves, bearing seedpods and grass plumes, some to lodge, some to move on. As the human clomps toward the streambend pool the first waterstriders of the season move their own shadows . . . then a silt disturbance . . . a form shoots squidlike to new rock cover . . . a crawfish . . . and one can realize what the heron knows and the human must scramble to discover.

Fred Waage

1811—John Jacob Astor's fur trading agents reach mouth of Columbia River

April 13   **DOMESTICATION**

Up here by Buffalo Mountain, the first green *is* gold, a field of gold, hard to know whether a field of death or promise. Horses graze in the high tension cut. The exhausted sun drowses, the Dr. Enuf trucks buzz on their runs. It is all undecided back home. The lillies are hanging on their own cross of semi-resurgence. Down by the road the red electric man in his red truck is messing around a pole—will the artifice of energy hold up or be swept away? It's warm enough to mulch and weed a few more gardens, even the lavender so thickly grown, undaunted. Collies love to watch humans at work. Branna licks sweaty heads. Even Tam Lin, his skin scales so dramatically reduced, paces the rails to inspect. We are all domesticated, we need fear only much greater disasters than these.

> "Ahead of me it was dark, but I could see the dogs' glistening fur. We were sledding in noonlight. A needle was slipped into my vein. Atropine . . . Blackness prevailed. The dogs who rescued me had dark fur. The dogsled carried me back into the day." Gretel Ehrlich, **A Match to the Heart** (1994)

April 14   **ENERGY**

Heavy rain and more to come. The clouds break briefly. There is more restoration from the freeze: tall buttercups have invaded the lawns, a texture of brightness, power of endurance, all summer mown, in a week show faces again. Further back, in more brushy terrain, their relatives the hooked buttercup, wide serrated leaves, coyer flowers. We nose wet trail back toward the Nameless Stream, free, still, of poison ivy. Muscular tree roots embracing the jagged rock face always astonish, the slow power of their grasp. Down here white stonecrop flowers adorn moss walls, unfrozen iris still blooms. The woodchuck cave remains sealed. Here the spring gushes perpetually out an unseemly black pipe, another broken pipe segment lies on the sand and pebbles, overtaken by watercress. Like the roots, the spring is implacable force, fixed in place, like cat Ki, "inner energy."

Sinking Creek Journal

1972—California Aqueduct begins operation

April 15   **STEADY RAIN**

    A church bell rings through the slow and steady rain, a chickadee chirps inside a wet bush. Drops pock birdbath and sundial. Collapsed tulips become sodden lumps. New maple leaves quiver and dance tap. Driveway puddles are boiling. Dead wisteria leaves hang and wave, braided strands. Indoor plants outside gleaming, human occupancy dust washed away. From shelter, a moving veil pacifies every organic outline. Jangled thicket around wisteria, squirrel-spilled feeder, sunflower-seeded splotch of wet earth, towhee, big rusty fox sparrows scratch for fallen seeds, dart into tangle and back. They have their own domestic space: food, shelter, brimming birdbath. They know no other life.

"In the evening I walked out over the fields to feel the soaked ground under my feet and smell the odors rising from the warm, wet earth in pasture, alfalfa, corn, and oat fields. Even the dogs seemed to enjoy the experience, barking and playing wildly." Louis Bromfield, **Malabar Farm** *(1948)*

April 16   **WHITE-OUT**

    Neighboring fields are white—fallen apple petals, white violets, ice-clumps mingle in the tall grass. Cold rising wind the morning after the latest Tennessee snow in memory. In shelter, wide window watching, all day rain visibly thickens, thickens, decelerates, over an hour, 38°, becomes dense thick snowbillows across freshly-minted linden and box elder leaves. Southwest the valley is whited out. After a stay, the snow begins to collect, fills tulip cups, grazes, then thickens over grass. The human eye focused on tree outlines experiences an undifferentiated sheet of white, brief snowflake sight plane, sharply-edged flash-life for each against undifferentiated green. Where no leaf purchase, the snow clumps on branches and thunks the roof. Sinking Creek itself, through this veil, is boiling brown, working hard. The fall is so discordant, so dramatic, it demands attention, and one gazes, meditational and entranced, on the performance.

1773—William Bartram leaves Savannah on botanical expedition

April 17   **HAWK HEAVEN**

It's hawk heaven, seemingly, sunny and breezy, and wings pass above—broad wing fully extended, distinctive white tail band, then shooting across the pine border, the low sun, blue-grey tone, long tapered wings. No other raptor save the peregrine has pointed wings, yet one hesitates to be sure, so unlikely are they in this space. All the creatures seem to come out as the cold lifts. Squirrels trash the feeders, but it's hard to have hard feelings, even for the crow picking a center line squirrel kill while three other living squirrels hover near. A bumblebee samples the fading phlox; blackeyed susan leaves freed of vinca's embrace emerge, a long ways yet to their bloom time.

"Now I lie back with half closed eyes and try to realize that I am at the bottom of another ocean—an ocean of air on which the hawks are sailing." Rachel Carson, *"Road of the Hawks"* (1945)

April 18   **MOTH HIGHWAY**

Tent caterpillars, prolific by the creek before, have been absent for many years now. They can be remembered as the paternal curse, objects of constant chemical revenge. Here their thick web nests between branches were simply, ecologically, bludgeoned to death. But the species need not fear extinction. Every tree, it seems, along the four-lane, even before leafing flaunts their white clumps. These are the trees beyond the grassed and mowed border. Their caterpillars will be fully matured eating machines just in time to greet each tree's tender emerging leaves. One asks why they are so prolific here, so scarce by the creek? But the freeway is a straight and open creek itself, sterilized of impediments, for many species a habitat severer, but this open passage is also a moth highway, the flight from tree to tree unimpeded; for the caterpillars, ecotone become healthy ribbon habitat (as its surface is for machines that eat the air).

Sinking Creek Journal

*1977—President Carter calls energy conservation
"the moral equivalent of war"*

April 19   **REFUGEES**

    Elephant ears have been indoors all winter, bending to the glass their broad leaves that look like—well, elephant ears. Some have not made it, some have root-joined offspring. You never know, though, when you put them out in May—the most unpromising root stubs still have fibers of life. Today, though, a new habitat has displayed itself. As the ears are watered, one long planter sprouts ants, ants upon ants, bearing pupae, a mad rush for the rim; how would one know until its forced dispersal that this settled community existed? Where will we go? Many, a photon swarm become a spreading beam, climb up the curved drusina spikes: the drusina has already been watered. In human terms the hand with the watering can has created a tide of refugees and almost anywhere safe is for them an alien terrain of grainless flat surfaces. But ants, after all! This is not Baghdad. Yet who can deny responsibility for the destruction of home space? As is said of warfare, the best way to kill them off is to destroy their nest.

1987—Last wild California Condor captured

April 20   **CLEARING**

    It has to be Spring when the mockingbirds dive-bomb the slow joe crows. The crows stick together—a patch of white on leaf cover suggests they spent last night in the trees right above. More palatable whitenesses now are the stonecrops' stars in every cranny. Ominous, though, is the semiaural air vibration, intensifying as we climb the hill. Faye cocks her ears, keeps returning for assurance that we really want to approach that sound. Scent of exhaust betrays that the homestead clearers have returned. This time there's a yellow pickup, a deep blue bobcat, and a large yellow tree-trunk lifter.

    "Hey, d'you know what's going in here?" "Well, bud, hear he's gonna put in a pond, not sure though." A pond? A private fishing preserve? A bathing spot? A cattle pond? Where will the water come from? Trucked

Fred Waage

in? Airlifted? There are no feeder streams on the farmstead. But any kind of pond beats a condo.

1832—Congress establishes the Arkansas Hot Springs Reservation

April 21   **VOYEUR**

This is about being on your home land but at a distance from the part of it you usually inhabit. A voyeur from without, from the edge of the forest, say. There are the lawn, the vehicles, the gardens, the wall photos half-seen through a half-open door. You are the only thing missing to center your realm of familiarity. Your own earth is under your feet but you are absent from your place. Your absence rings through you like a low bell, a passing bell . . . you are drawn to return, but you are still there. This half-acre green triangle across the creek is the locus of this paradox. The curtain of green has not fully closed, but the tumbling stream is an ocean. There on the other side is Leif with his tennis ball, wondering where his master has gone. Turn away. Half of this triangle is mowed, separated from its neighbor's only because it is rougher, not torched by anti-weed pollutants. There's a fabled, unused, volleyball net, a circular garden colorless save for yellow loosestrife. The triangle's upper third is a woodland in progress, left to evolve, somewhat as a memorial to the magnificent deceased elm, whose burial mound centers it . . . On the trail maintained through this growing woods, the strangeness of absence feels strongest. Shrouded in leaves, creek at his feet, the savage outlier can yet almost touch the wall of his own secure bedroom.

1827—Broken levee launches Mississippi Flood of 1827

April 22   **HEATING UP**

It's really heating up now, everywhere leaves are unfurling, phallic sumac torches, red maple saplings by the hundreds, gold Virginia creeper leaves canopied down, then rising and spreading, but beware the new poison ivy leaves, same color, different shape, filling out too. (The collies, who were bathed and groomed just in time, and given their tummy tuxedo cuts cool those tummies in the Nameless Stream). The commonest understory trees are the baby pignut hickories, just starting out, predoomed by shade unless some of their elders, their parents even, fall. They scatter the trail, thin pointed ovate leaves barely toothed reddish. Many of them are also reddened by tube galls, miniature spiky lipstick cylinders, clustered on their leaves. These galls are species-specific: only the hickories have them; they will not kill, will release eventually the growing insect-deposited young life within them.

1889—Oklahoma land rush begins at noon

April 23   **AIR FULL**

Not a cloud, the upper air is full—of insects, invisible to grounded mortal eyes but not to the swifts which, violently poetic, flutter and hurtle, wings curved like strung bows, little caffeinated vultures, crossing in group but not interactive chase . . . and then the hawks, oblique redtails, crossing against the sun, driven wingbeats, seen through the pin oak newly gold . . . and bluejay power, everywhere chatters and hoots, tribes of goldfinches, tiger swallowtails, cardinals clashing midair to claim the papal throne, higher yet noisy biplanes, rescue helicopters, below, flies in the house, falling seedfluff, exploratory wasps, birdshadows passing . . .

"I can almost feel, myself, the outer primary feathers extended like sensitive fingers, constantly adjusting to air currents, and that delicate edge of blending, where the motion of the electron of the feathers and htose of the air merge into the thing called flight." Susan Cerulean, **Tracking Desire** *(2006)*

April 24   **STRIVERS**

Every hollowed rotting stump cups moss at least, if not a full-fledged maidenhair fern. There's a sudden tiny colony of mountain shamrock (more commonly known as wood sorrel, *oxalis violacea*), with round clovery leaf clusters and a five-petaled purple bloom atop each discrete stem. This *oxalis* colony is a minority here in white violet territory. Around it are the wild iris, the trout lily leaves, the latter long unflowered but now trailing redundant oval pinkish seed capsules—redundant since the plants spread mainly from underground corms. A large, long, debranched pine has bisected the trail, bearing down with it the living and the dead, Virginia creeper crawling over it still alive. The fall of the pine cannot kill the vine. Comfrey flower stalks have risen and their flowers, still furry clumps. Many golden unfurling low leaves that seemed like poison ivy two days ago are now revealed as elm saplings, and the spear-shaped leaf buds of many other baby trees strive, while their earlier frost-killed mates hang, like white ghosts.

1957—Albert Schweitzer's Declaration of Conscience on Nuclear Radiation

April 25   **REJECTEES**

The sole observable ungroomed land around the spreading VA hospital is a single waste strip pressed between the railroad cut's stony slope and Brush Creek, soupily flowing behind banks (the money type) . . . mustard, honeysuckle, countless castoff containers. Standing in these stunted weeds you can hear cars grinding gears over the tracks and into the VA grounds, the mocking quacks of government ducks safe in their government-issued duckpond with its two fake fountains. Spring seems to have excluded this strip, as the military did its evicted human inhabitants—an organized encampment of vets excluded from the groomed grounds. About a decade ago the cops moved in, dispersed the *sans papiers*. Surely, however, it remains a nocturnal refuge for the homeless and venal—fresh trash testifies to that—and for the foragers, raccoons, rats, and then the foragers upon these, the foxes who come slumming here on moonless nights.

1952—Watson and Crick publish description of double helix

April 26   **PLEASURE IN PREDATION**

Tam Lin, with the help of steroid shots, has almost completely recovered from his woodchuck wounds. Only two crusted pink patches remain on his throat, and they shrink steadily. He is enjoying being a cat again. And there is proof: this hot afternoon he paces the back walk confidently,

Sinking Creek Journal

a towhee between his jaws. The beautiful chestnut-sided towhee's exaggerated seed-scratching has caught up with him. All this is saddening to the human sensibility, but not to the feline. Here is a species-defined perceptual barrier: the feline's announcement of restored health is to the human a tragic predation; the tragic near death of the feline resulted from his predatory urge. Predation thus has marked the beginning and ending of this life-phase for Tam Lin. The human, more evolved, can only wait on the sidelines and weep. But, back in front, behold, scratching at sunflower seeds, another chestnut-sided towhee, just a much smaller one than the backyard victim. So fecundity fights predation.

1986—Chernobyl nuclear disaster

April 27   **GARBAGE**

Now the first trout fingerlings maneuver the streambend pond. Blue skippers and hairstreaks dance in open woods. Between the streamside trail and the abandoned pumping station's graffitied back, an entire bag of household garbage has been strewn amid the whitely purple fleabane. From its bourbon-dominated contents, one can see it's not *our* garbage, and suspicion turns not to human litterers but to any number of large quadrupeds capable of dragging such a succulent treasure to sample in this private place. Maybe a new generation of black bears has revived last Spring's foraging. Turn your back on the garbage, O my people! Seat yourselves where the great beech trunk curves comfortably, the new chinquapin leaves spread downward, and observe how the clear, spring-fed, fishscale-waved stream flows silently over sienna sands.

Arbor Day

April 28
Carnegie, PA   **BRIDGES IN THE MIST**

The gilt onion domes of the Russian Orthodox churches are blue here, this old factory city's emblematic color, as are the signs and pylons along its "historic" main street, reaching for revival. American primitive hometown hero Honus Wagner stares fiercely at all newcomers from his brick-wall prison. It seems strange that the Hero and the Founder are both rooted in this minor space—particularly the latter, considering the industrial grandeur and defilement he wrought upon the American land. Of course steel and athletes are historically the Monogahela Valley's most prominent products, this rough and ridged Northern Appalachian terrain somehow welded to horizontals, verticals. A chill, misty rain engorges all the Golden Triangle's sleek skyscrapers, hollow-eyed brick factories, multi-rusted bridges. The Monongahela is a vision of bridges from somewhere to nowhere, bridges in the mist . . .

1958—Linus Pauling predicts massive genetic defects, cancers as result of atomic fallout

April 29 **FISHERBOY**

A car has pulled onto our triangle across the stream. Through the trees we see a flurry of color, clatter of fill stones. The collies in full cry toward the intrusion. Down the gentle slope on our side (once, long ago, children's "sandy beach") a young woman looks up, a little excited-eyed boy with her, his tiny fully-equipped fishing pole—float, sinker—in the pool under our bridge. "Are you fishing?" "Yes." "Sure, go right ahead." Collies dance back. It seems once they know the Master approves, they assume their defensive services are no longer needed. What about fishing? All little males who've had some nature contact love it—is it indigenous to them, a survival-imprinted activity? One could ask, if this little boy can have his pop-tarts, why does he still want, or need, to fish? Of course, this is ridiculous. Sandra Day O'Connor loves to fish. The excitement of predation is primal. The ecopuritan has no standing in this matter. Son Erick was non-puritanically allowed to play with toy soldiers. He was obsessed with them. Now he's a real soldier. What quadrupredator would not teach its offspring the arts of survival? It would be against nature for the bipredator not to do so.

> "*A big blue bird
> watches from branches,
> above,
> as I try to think like the fish
> I want to catch
> who waits in the darkest part
> of the river
> for its last meal.*"
> Thomas Rain Crowe, **Zoro's Field** (2005)

April 30   **HEAT AND GROWTH**

So the cruelest month comes to an end in a blast of heat and growth. Little red buds dot all the Franklinia's little branches. Brighter green tufts end each hemlock sprig. Plump black woodland salamander, solitary jack-in-the-pulpit, powder blue comfrey flower bunches unfolded now. Even the trucks on the ex-farmstead have not been able to obliterate the pink lady slippers: beneath a group of raddled Virginia pines there's a colony of them, one sensuous pink pouch, others rising up. Lady slippers metabolize soil nutrients through the agency of a fungus that grows only on pine roots. Therefore, they cannot be transplanted or potted. Because they are so visible, they are steadily being lost to Appalachian forests. Hopefully on this mixed-growth high tract there are other colonies further back which can thrive unnoticed.

1803—Louisiana Purchase finalized

May 1   **ENCOUNTERS**

May Day. Steaming hot. The mower marks two "first" encounters while executing buttercups: bog frog escape, a hail mary bogleap; first praying mantis, safe beneath yucca spears, yet a nymph, half-inch long, but distinct triangular head. This mantis will go through many metamorphoses as the summer passes; sex is fate, matriarchal mantids make males dead meat, though these females, powerful in September green glory and intelligence, will be doomed by the cold. Unconcerned with time, the ancient crabapple tree blooms heavily pink, its arthritic limbs festooned with color. Beneath it the dandelions all have white heads now. The benevolent mower explodes the heads and spreads the parachuted seeds among apple blossoms, throughout the crabapple's empire. After the coming rain, how many more yellow heads will rise, turn white, be dispersed by the machine in the garden?

*1958—Coast Guard seizes anti-nuclear
protest ship* Golden Rule *near Hawaii*

May 2   **FLAT CREEK**

Two notorious beer joints have been transformed respectively into a day care center and a sexy lingerie store, "Intimate Treasures." The multi-acre junkyard becomes incomprehensible sculpture rust-garden that would warm Janisse Ray's heart. "Yankee Salvage"—dedicated to salvaging Yankees? Miles of urban sprawl, a misty azure Tennessee agriscape, barns, cattle, winding roads, groves, stream-rich . . . and, behold, twenty miles south another Sinking Creek. This one does not bound in a rush, but rather a slow deep South flat moving over plated rocks, beside real gabled farmhouses with porches, field dogs and tractors, drooping willows that deserve Spanish moss, mowed borders and metal chairs, two blanket women gossiping, bare-torsoed farmer bearing naked baby, wild fields and plowed, immense brooding abandoned mill, Purina symbol, "weed and feed." The village of Afton, post office, Henderson's Mill built here 1798, first white baby born "hereabouts." Hereabouts the streams move slowly, one realizes despite it all the great underdeveloped middle landscape interior . . . think perhaps, hopefully, the sprawl is deceptively thin . . . grazing lands, then . . . crash: right on the rural 2-lane an immense modern high school.

*1974—Congress legislates a Federal Energy
Administration to be established by July, 1975*

Sinking Creek Journal

May 3   **CUCUMBER TREE**

    The cucumber tree (*magnolia acuminata*) blossoms are falling like fat yellow raindrops. All summer its bowing branches, great ovate leaves, cover all the yard front, so it can shelter a stone freestanding patio and a shade garden shaped like its shadow. Later in the summer its cucumber seedpods and scarlet seeds will fall in these same spaces. It has a dignified conical symmetry, and fills all the space of light. According to the Tennessee Vascular Plants Database, it does not grow in our county, but this cucumber tree is undeniably real. It is so imposing it's hard to believe that in its youth its trunk was small enough to tie the (now deceased) collies' leashes 'round, leaving a groove of bondage now long overgrown.

International Migratory Bird Day

May 4   **SHELTER**

    The roofers are busy next door, refurbishing a nest, as lightning approaches. In John Steuart Curry's great painting, "The Line Storm," the hay wagon gallops barnward, ahead of a moving curtain: clouds and violent light. One considers the security of basic human needs like food and shelter, and how distanced many of us have become from the sources that fulfill these needs. The neighbors are not replacing their own roof, nor did they construct its components with their own hands from materials grown, gleaned, elaborated by their own hands (no more did Gilgamesh, of course, hew his own stone and raise his own palace). The hay gleaners and the roofers move toward the same immediate goal, of course—shelter. Only, in the painting, it is the gleaners' products that must be gotten to shelter, for future use. The neighbors need shelter for themselves and the products they have mainly purchased from intermediary sources; these products are already under their roof. Yet the distance here may be more apparent than real—in the present case survival hangs by one thread, one wire, one power grid, on chain of electrical connections, maybe thus even more vulnerable than the haywagon fleeing, the foaming horses.

Fred Waage

*1956—The Atomic Energy Commission
authorizes private atomic energy plants*

May 5   **OPENING THE DOOR**

    Now the neighbors are having a deck, a big deck, constructed; the humans constructing it exchange animal sounds, create a verbal cooperative web. Another construction project is also going on, with only two constructors: one materials gatherer, one construction supervisor. This project creates an environmental quandary for the Human in Charge, since it is actually a squatters' project. The male house wren gathers organic threads from the lining of a yet-to-be-filled hanging basket, transports them to and through a very narrow gap above the toolshed door. The female wren presumably arranges them as she sees fit, since soon both wrens appear, perch atop the door, even flit to the roof peak. Ownership is all. But what if the Human in Charge opens the door? What if the nest is being constructed atop a "necessary" tool? Who is really in charge here? Does one species' convenience outweigh another's necessity?

> "Above the roar
> hear the song of the canyon wren."
> Gary Snyder, "The Canyon Wren"

May 6   **FECUNDITY**

    Three days of rain ended this morning, leaving sparkles on newly leafed hyssop, overbearing beebalm, newly blooming deep purple columbine, white wild cherry, purple lyre sage. In these days more pink lady slippers emerge, the comfrey begins to fade out. Planting vegetables in the raised bed across the stream means the purple vetch controlling it must be ethnically cleansed, except for one token corner. Vivid and subtle, an indigo bunting passes through; there are many millipedes on the rock slope, perhaps rained out of their lairs. White tailed dragonfly coursing the stream freezes, perfectly camouflaged, hopefully prophesies a rich insect summer. Even the butterfly bushes, so frost-devastated, now sprout leaves at every stipule, soon will become again the insects' Local.

Sinking Creek Journal

> ". . .our hair
> turns white with our ripening
> as though to fly away in some
> coming wind, bearing the seed
> of what we know . . ."
>   Wendell Berry, "Ripening"

May 7   **BERRIES**

    White blackberry bloom arcs, bows, begins to rainbow over lawns, visual whitewater cascades. Blackberries, *rubus alleghaniensis*, have an annunciatory role in temperate zones—or else create one. They are the first strike invaders of clear lawns, pawns in the game, enablers ultimately disabled by the shade they promoted. There are 122 species of blackberries. Those growing at high elevations lack thorns. Unfortunately, down here they're full-thorned, protected from humans, but fortunately provide nutrition for a wide variety of bees, flies, butterflies. There are two other blackberry relatives on our property. Up above, a black raspberry colony, similar canes, fruit cupped, not pointed. By the drive red raspberries emerged last year, fast growing, thick red canes, thorns thin as hairs. "Trained," trimmed, their fruit looks much sweeter than that which decays under supermarket plastic, but—alas!—it is bitter to the human, eye candy without sugar. They should be left for other predators, whose tastes are less confined, who can spread their seeds more widely.

1888—George Eastman patents Kodak box camera

May 8   **UPSTREAM**

    Walking Sinking Creek upstream. Phlox have oval seedpods. Witch hazel heart-shaped leaves line stream. Poison ivy ascendant. The road has many uphill dead-end tributaries; one, blocked now, used to pierce a hay barn center; rusty rails remain of its bridge. Many traditional one-story porched wooden houses: doghouse, outboard, motorcycle. Sad-eyed woman waves from one of three dingy trailers. New log house leers down

Fred Waage

ridge through trees. Elms, white pines, chinquapins, ash-maples, umbrella magnolias. Wider closecropped lawns: mockingbird and robin territory. This newer wide bridge deterred endemic flooding at the point where road and stream cross each other. Creeper-buried outbuilding of house spectacularly burned in the 80s. Berea Church, clean, white. New and ancient stream retention walls. Stream on right buries itself in foliage, rockface rises, going uphill, road crosses stream again, valley widens, pasture, stream treeline moves away, Buffalo Mountain ridge lost in soft perspective.

1879—George Selden files first patent application for a gas-run car

May 9   **NURSERY SOCIOLOGY**

Addiction to the Nursery resembles addiction to the Bookstore, but buying what you will never read is different from buying what you will never plant. A life is at stake. This commercial nursery is dependent on polluting chemicals, the very killers it displays for sale on its shelves. The Nursery in Spring is a layered hierarchy of desire. Outdoors are the absurdities of garden sculpture, the hanging baskets of short life-expectancy, the water garden plants and tubs of koi. Then the jangly novelties, the invisible wall of garden chemicals you must pass through to reach hyperoxygenated ranks upon rank of real plants. Even these, tented, have a depth hierarchy—the further you go, the more serious you are: indoor exotics yield to group-display annuals, to freestanding annuals, to veggies, herbs off in a corner, and finally the really earnest guys, the perennials. Behind this circus in other off-limit 120° tents, plants are prepared by triage for display, and seeds punched, endless finger thrusts, to germinate. Out in the wasteland of this former farm the week, feeble, rootbound unsold are dumped to congeal. At night the feral cats come down hillsides in military formation to gorge on the nursery's vermin. When Ginger worked at the nursery she won the prize for finding the largest slug in a pot.

"The garden . . . is the inner landscape projected."
Paul Shepard, **Traces of an Omnivore** (1996)

Sinking Creek Journal

May 10   **BIRDVASION**

    May Appalachian afternoon, light breeze stirs leaftips; except for breathing, illusion of eternity . . . clouds flow east, crows fly west . . . drowsy propellers, high up Newark-Atlanta jet trails. A birdvasion: cardinal feeds wife, hypocritical red-headed woodpecker bill-jousts brown thrasher in sunflower seed-patch, drives it off, then hops up magnolia, pretends to be working, hops down for free ground food, hops up again. No one is fooled. Grackles are back, their rice-crispies grak call, boat tails and iridescent sharkskin suits, blue heads. Full sun . . . wavering stillness . . . power saws . . . life glistens . . .

1869—Transcontinental Railroad completed at Promontory Point

May 11   **HAND AND PLANT**

    There is no Final Solution. Unweeding this groundcover slope by the bog, by hand, is but a temporary setback for the deportees. They'll weave their way in again, under and through . . . But Final Solutions threaten life. They are usually chemical solutions. Everyone dies. So the trowel is wielded in a dance, fingers reaching into dirt, unlacing racemes, cupping rootbunches. Even thus the threatened cultivars are accidentally pulled out from time to time. The natural bindweed, grasses, fleabane root clumps are so artfully enmeshed with the roots of artifice that sometimes there is no separating them. But still the best tool for planting or uprooting remains the ungloved hand. The hand's neural branches are attuned to the plant's branching roots and changing textures of its soil. The more tactile education it receives, the more subtly can the hand and plant, even when antagonists, collaborate. Too many hands have been estranged from the earth, too many seek Final Solutions in the featureless pressure on the trigger, on the button, on the keyboard.

1950—President Truman dedicates the Grand
Coulee Dam on the Columbia River

May 12 **PERSIAN VIOLET**

Erick has sent his mother a Persian Violet plant, *exacum affine*, for Mother's Day. As he is graduating West Point on May 26, probably headed for the Middle East, this is a sweet and sour gift. *Exacum* has exuberant purple flowers with yellow centers. It is native to Socotra ("Isle of Bliss") off the coast of Yemen. Socotra is a paradise of unique, and therefore endangered, species, the other hemisphere's Galapagos. So the Persian violet is a paradox, named for one politically problematic nation but actually native to another, while representing the apolitical fecundity of nature, expressed in motherhood. But on this day and time it is a *memento mori*, symbolically appropriated by culture. Only in this individual situation can the Persian violet flourish, like its flowers, so many purely human messages.

"If beauty is locked into the booths of static criteria, it becomes self-conscious, it no longer is beauty. It is dead. If we lose beauty, we have nowhere to take our pain." Maggie Ross, ***Seasons of Death and Life*** *(1990)*

May 13 **NEW GROWTH**

Just enough rain yesterday to permeate the soil. Sandals covered with buttercup petals. Multiflora roses blooming white. First goldenrod on sunny hillsides. New ragwort, also yellow, by stream. Milkweed stalks starting out. Ragweed invasions becoming serious. Cats fighting in the parsley bed. New Franklinia leaves at last. Virginia creeper creeps over the front door. Blooming watercress mounded high. Beebalm will bloom soon—needs powdery mildew medication. Two subtle columbine tints now. New tulip poplar, box elder saplings to protect erosion-prone streamside. Long dogmessage barking the valley.

1908—*Theodore Roosevelt authorizes a National Conservation Commission*

May 14 **POND OF DREAMS?**

Well, it sure looks like a "pond" is going down at the base of the Bastian farmstead. The bulldozer is gearing up, crows protest. There's a deep rectangle, roughly fifty feet wide, ending in a high, flat-surfaced dam,

Sinking Creek Journal

so from it one looks unnaturally far down onto the familiar trail. Sections of 6-inch plastic pipe lie about, there's a pile of gravel and one strip that resembles heavy pond liner. Still the question of whither the water. The bare earth is dry. A human tornado has touched down and lifted. There are no good witches here. What matters it that downslope the delicate white toothwort cups have emerged? So what will the summer bring to someone's pond of dreams?

1804—Lewis and Clark set out

May 15   **LEAF SHADOWS**

What we call the "power spot," a boulder seat/step where the springflow, creek, Nameless Stream converge between mountain and flowing water. From here leaves block the view of every house, only the weimaraner's bark betrays it. Prestorm humid heat and growing wind shielded out here. Collies walk on water. Leaf undersides are blown back, leafshadows on other leaves. Massive triune oak-hickory trunks entwist each other, a decades-old embrace for light. Drifting maple leaf shadows animate the page where immobile words are rooted. Faye contemplates too, her lapped ears perk forward at every sound. Gusts are heavier now, seedpods descend. The forest speaks, we hear but do not understand. Returning, Branna noses another seasonal first, an immature box turtle, light brown markings on darker.

1862—President Lincoln establishes Department of Agriculture

May 16   **POND OF DREAMS**

Uncultivated fields, farmyard condos, trailer parks, machine shops, rolling pastures. Amid them, exurban Willow Springs Park falling downhill, curvaceous paths, canting women swinging unison children, rheumatic dogs and pooper scoopers, purple clover, plaintain, paintbrush. At the bottom, a real springfed pond, as it should be, one side bushed, the other all cattails, tops defluffing. Dark clouds are coming in, its water is ridged. A map turtle slides off a log. Everywhere, red-winged blackbirds, shoulders of scarlet felt, spraying tails, teetering on reeds, their persistent calls—deep gurgles and aural reeds drawn to a point. They balance close, as though tamed, encompass the pond, weave all its constituents into a song. There's a "raft" floating—childwork?—stick rectangle tied together with cattail stems, human handwork as from a depth of time, floating on the surface of the present.

1910—Congress authorizes a Bureau of Mines

May 17   **DANGEROUS ADAPTATION**

Cool morning follows late afternoon downpour. Wet leaves and spider webs. It is said today that avian flu has decimated U.S. bird populations, especially our common "homebirds"—crows, chickadees, tufted titmice. Social, they interact around built areas, at feeders, near standing water: their very adaptation to human presence endangers them. Is this not a truth of environmental history—our species kills what it loves as well as what it hates. Yet, nonetheless, ferns are still turgid, undergrowth saplings aspire. The squawroot has found new life, its spiky brown stems like living bottlebrushes rise where oaks grow, it is "bear corn." Earthen track up to the pond site has been gravelled, but untouched beside it yet another new lady slipper, with more to come.

1864—Congress transfers Yosemite Valley from the public domain to the State of California

May 18   **THROUGH QUAKER KNOBS**

To the left, Rich Mountain flows blue, shadows itself. At Reahtown—one general store—then up Jockey Road, signs warn drivers of farm machinery, orange blazing stars in every yard, cattle, and elderly bonneted woman hoeing, purple phacelia. All these small farms are below Quaker Knobs, a curved line of teton-esque hills, where Quakers settled in the eighteenth century, producing Elihu Embree, publisher of the first abolitionist newspaper. The Knobs are hardwood—oak, maple—and a branch of the "other" Sinking Creek flows through the Gap of the Knobs where

Sinking Creek Journal

suddenly farmland is gone, woods surround, dark, and miniature waterfalls, then suddenly again, bright sun, again Sinking Creek Road, this one not traveled, authentically rural, one-laned, crunching gravel, it rises a brushy hill, great oak in a field by the diminished stream, harrowing farmer, half-naked kids, one stern out-of-place brick foursquare house, one abandoned one, you can look straight through its empty windows to the abandoned barn behind. Now almost a track, the road trickles finally down to a slightly wider one and the Handle Bars Inn, surrounded, of course, by motorcycles.

1933—Tennessee Valley Authority established

May 19   **PROPHECIES**

The return to the childhood home after long absence is a cultural motif as ancient as the *Odyssey*—but an intimately known place can change drastically to the inhabitant's perception even after a short absence. Looking out over our green realm before such an absence, one can of course predict the implacable growth of grass and weeds. The seed-babies—calendula, leek, dill, oregano, basil—will have risen toward planting size. Ivy will have spread, peonies bloomed, new mint reencroached the kitchen garden. Faye will have eaten more of the lemon grass. Angles and duration of light and shade will have subtly changed with the shifting earth. And the invisible life will have momentously altered—new births, new deaths of plants, insects, birds—in a wake the Place will be, beneath the veil of Same, actually changed, changed utterly, in all except its beauty.

> *"In her memory, the horizon had been so much wider, the road so much longer, the band of woods so much deeper. It seemed to her that the landscape must have diminished in an incredible way since she had left it." Ellen Glasgow,* **Barren Ground** *(1925)*

May 20
Shenandoah Valley, VA   **TRAFFIC**

Cloud shadows on the Blue Ridge, black shadows of black cattle on green pasture, a pasture full of cows and tottering calves. High Victorian gables on the highway, truncated estates and symmetrical white-fenced cupolaed brick mansions, abandoned hayracks, slow tree-swathed river branches crossed and recrossed by teetering loads of new tin cars, interchange encrustations. NEW MARKET, CEDAR CREEK—where once a Spring invasion ravaged a valley in one savage swoop, so springs later another, more lastingly destructive one which continues 24 hours a day, day after day, year after year.

1862—Lincoln signs the Homestead Act

May 21
Piscataway NJ   **ECOCHANGES**

"Garden State" is an overused irony. "I'm from Jersey." "Oh yeah? Which exit?" "Garden" a century ago was as in "truck garden," i.e., agriculture. North and Central New Jersey were New York City's farm. Over the twentieth century the agricultural land was bought by developers and grew innumerable "ranch" style houses, encompassing old village and town centers. Often you can drive a development and find in its center an anomalous house of two stories and a peaked roof, on higher ground—the original farmhouse, remodeled into nonentity. For example, this acre here was part of a new 1960s street-length dead-end development, piercing farmland. Construction photos show it on naked pared ground, barns in the distance. Forty years later it and its peers are relics. Even in the 80s you could go to the dead end and you'd be looking out over working dairy farms, fields of cattle and sweet manure. Now these farms are gone, replaced by million-dollar shoulder-separated mansions on postage stamps. The New Jersey Nets play in a massive field house right there, across Metlars Lane. But, fatal irony, this acre, yesterday's intrusion, is today's refuge. Since its Master has died, the internal brush has been piled at its forsythia edges, overgrown, its lawn is cleared, shaded but bright. Phalanxes of robins, doves, squirrels parade and joust all day. Catbirds nest on warped fruit trees. Deer trace down the suburban interstitial mazes to graze on its protected lawn. Today, chilly, weeks "behind" southern Appalachia, three fox kits dance and stalk at its far border. Their ears prick like cats', they're brown, keen-eyed, tails trail black to white at the tip. Freedom to Desecration to Refuge.

Sinking Creek Journal

❦

1956—*First airborne explosion of a fusion bomb, at Bikini*

May 22
Piscataway NJ   **VIXEN**

    Latino beats to hammer strokes backscore robins' trolling, and abrasive brushclearing saws, green inchworm mobiles on filaments. Don, next door: really cold these days, inchworms eating hell outa the trees, been to Tennessee, Pigeon Forge, Memphis; seen the foxes, likes them. This yard is truly a vulpine preserve. At 8 AM a twenty-first century vixen and five kits cavort around the birdbath, up real close, play hide-and-seek all afternoon, scratching, luxuriating full length on tummies, rolling on backs, sharp-eared batfaces still attuned to human presence. In fact, perusing Piscataway on wheel and foot seems to show it less overpopulated than it has seemed. Swaths of acreage in scrap wood second growth. All Ginger's old youth haunts built over but also tree-overgrown. Tourelled *nouveau* manor house in a swamp. Lilacs galore. Mustard-yellow rabbit fields. The Cornell Dairy's 30+ acre bony horse trampled eyesore next to Piux X High School—muddy houses, "riding lessons," decades old—its houses are now boarded, horses gone, grass regrowing: "Future Community Park." Future—how far? NO OUTLET the culs-de-sac say. Are they truthtellers? The only human tenant of the vulpine acre is old now, her life hangs by a thread as thin as that which holds the only unfallen wind-chime tube, rotating silently with its pendulum. When that last tube falls, will there be a human to take care of this refuge? A custodian? *Qui custoderit custodes?*

❦

1843—*First major wagon train to the
Northwest sets out on the Oregon Trail*

May 23
Montgomery NY   **SCENT OF HISTORY**

    Town of unwithered elms and Orange County Choppers—hay and gasoline. Looking up when the wind blows, the complex elm patterns more gloriously than any kaleidoscope. Scrawny kids with attitude skateboard past Revolutionary-era churches and storefronts. The pungent scent of History is outodored by the rancidity of schoolbus diesel. Lilacs bloom everywhere, boring bees still seek the right place to bore. "Ward's Mill" became Montgomery after the heroic general died at Québec and missed the Revolution. The ground around is porous, sedgy lakelets, waterlogged trees, semi-marsh clearings. English sparrows occupy the linden tree birdhouse, their nestlings' yellow bills poke out. The third graders, fledglings, race tricycles in front of the courthouse steps, they plant flowers throughout Historic Montgomery. Between here and the Hudson the New York Thruway roars.

1908—*National Bison Range established, Montana*

May 24
Fort Putnam,
West Point, NY   **ORGANIC FORM**

This was the second-highest fortified position at West Point during the Revolutionary War. The hot Spring Hudson valley steams far below, with Constitution Island, and across the river the castle where *The Wizard of Oz* was filmed. Above, the mountain is outcropped with rock, and, as common, bare trees killed by acid rain. From the air, in winter, the rock snow melts first, and Erick says the mountain then resembles a border collie. Fort Putnam's walls and batteries curve around and insinuate themselves within the steep, irregular, boulder-strewn terrain—organic form, and in this way very like the Point itself. For all its architecture's greystone Spartan order, it switchback climbs an implacable steepness, passage through it is all curve and flow, over two centuries it has shaped itself to the landscape's contours.

". . .of all the underlying forces working toward emancipation of the city dweller, most important is the gradual reawakening of the primitive instincts of the agrarian." Frank Lloyd Wright, **The Living City** *(1958)*

Sinking Creek Journal

May 25
The Plain,
West Point NY   **CONTROL**

 Crowds cheer, band marches, crowd applauds. Two little girls on the grass have adopted a tent caterpillar. It crawls the thongs of their sandals like roads, dutifully exits onto held out sticks . . . eventually they want to take it home. Absorbed in its movements, they're oblivious to the Real pomp and circumstance before them. Cadets collapse in the intolerable heat and rise again. The caterpillar also must have its own direction and purpose, but the human Others have forestalled them. The two little girls and the caterpillar present in miniature an environmental dilemma much greater in impact even than war itself. The species wills control of the non-human, control embedded, endemic, pre-ethical. It can be modified but not destroyed. And it is in the long term, inherently, self-destructive.

1900—The Lacey Act restricts wild bird commerce

May 26
Michie Stadium,
West Point NY   **SWALLOWS**

 The barn swallows skim low and high, insect-directed and indifferent to crowds, cadets, the Vice President himself. Focus on the swallows, watch them veer and bank, display their ruddy breasts, and above all their total indifference to the rituals of human concern, and you can get caught by their graceful nonchalance, lose for a moment consciousness that human Deep Import is enacting itself below. These are reservoir swallows, but surely the mass of sweating humanity cupped here today has attracted more insects to be swallowed than have the reservoir's misty waters. The swallow daringly clip dignitaries' heads, weave among generals; none of the sharpshooters, the men in black, blow them away, yet they are fully armed with an alternative consciousness. Later we maneuver the hot cottonwood snowstorm, fuzzy seeds fly and collect everywhere. They too are airborne and indifferent as Melville's swallows at Shiloh.

1952—Arctic National Wildlife Range Act

Fred Waage

May 27
Newburgh NY   **VULTURES OF URBANITY**

Tattoos; Gnostic Cult; *alcoholicos anonymos*; Irish Eyes Pub—private Police party; Sacred Heart Italian Feast; multiethnic soccer matches under looming skies. Newburgh seems much as it was ten years ago. On Broadway, the bombed-out Imperial Motel still rots. Front-porch row houses, some restored, some not. Downing Park—an elegant fountain pond filled with Canada geese: are those petals or goose droppings covering its waters? A pair of canners work their way up the street. The guy hauls a plastic bag of cans, the lady pushes a shopping cart. Canners, homeless, sell discarded containers to survive. They glean from dawn to dusk. Truckers gather the unreturned cans, bottles they collect, in the night, for less than the recyclers would pay. It says in Leviticus that every cultivator should leave corner space for the poor to plant their meager crops. So the canners should, or do, gather the meager offal of their plastic betters. They are cleaning the environment in their own way. Vultures of urbanity, they cruise on their own, but one may well, given the line of evolution from plastic water bottle to consumer to retailer to distributor to producer, ask why?

1935—Soil Conservation Act passed

May 28
Shippensburg PA   **GOD'S ACRE**

The Memorial Day parade is assembling to progress through the preserved downtown of this 1730 community. The colonially dressed girls, World War II vets, cluster under cemetery trees as sun beats down without mercy. Folks cluster the route and a fat lady distributes little American flags. Almost the entire assemblage is white. A black boy, arm in a sling, views it from the side. His t-shirt says HATE NOTHING FEAR NOTHING DO SOMETHING. A cultural ritual in remembrance of the past, particularly the military past, but as though the community celebrated has existed here forever, an eternal past. A generational ritual: kindergarten baton twirlers, staggering vets commingle; there is, and rightfully so, little nature in

Sinking Creek Journal

this picture. After the last EMS vehicle has passed, the lawn chairs are folded, older people wander and muse at monuments, flags, in the cool, tree-sheltered Episcopal cemetery, "DEDICATED TO THE PATRIOTS AND PIONEERS WHO SLEEP IN THIS GOD'S ACRE." God's acre. Patriots and Pioneers. More than any parade, this inscription combines all the factors defining mortal America.

1830—Andrew Jackson signs Indian Removal Act

May 29
Shenandoah Valley, VA   **ABANDON**

Abandoned (in this stretch of the valley): stone multi-arched bridge, its roadway long gone to grass; one large gas station, plateaued pump-covers; a half-dozen farmhouses: gaunt and bare, honeysuckle-overrun, pillared porches grey and pale; one schoolbus with white eyes; two gift shops; one motel; three Calvary crosses, Christ's tipped awkwardly; one cornfield centered by a Century 21 sign, others "zoned commercial;" a baby stroller; hubcaps; numerous truck tire rubber fillets, some with steel bands revealed, resembling blackened racks of lamb. Moving South without abandon, one notices increasing farm activity, lines of cattle salt licks, cultivators in motion. A return in mind to the tiers of displacement: Native Americans by settlers, plantations pillaged by Sheridan, the original valley highway, route 11, the Lee Highway, by the interstate, ironically named for primal white settler Andrew Lewis.

1843—John C. Frémont's major Western survey team leaves Kansas City

May 30   **BACK HOME**

Home is not the same, but not as different as it might have been, because of a weeklong drought. Collies moon with joy, cats stalk pretending indifference. Grass has grown little, the raspberry-red columbine has not faded. White allium clusters have replaced the blue orbs, there are yellow mullein bells, purple May night salvia spikes, tigrish oriental lilies, pink azaelia mass; all these are new to the eye, in the raised beds. Gladiola blades upthrust. A silence of birds, feeder dishabituated. The creek is fading, the trout maneuver its shrinking pools. Will it swell again before they drown in the air? Young veggies have survived the heat; parsnips must be thinned. The unregulated vegetation has thickened so there are scarcely any sightlines beyond it and threatens to overgrow the driveway itself—the illusion of privacy enhanced by all the nonhuman growing things that can witness our every move.

1986—First outdoor test of genetically altered plants

May 31   **HOPE OF RAIN**

And in the woods nothing new, just a great deal more of the same. All understory saplings have widened over the trail—beech, black cherry, hickories of every name. Even the dump seems to contain more junk. Spiderwebs galore—you can eyeball the spiders as you duck their constructions. Staghorn ferns all have high erections, but the farmstead "pond" seems unchanged from its primitive graded state, waiting for rain. Almost 90° yesterday, today cloud-darkened, humidified in, horseflies tease heads. Black cohosh fixing to flower. Pileated woodpecker more noisy than usual. Everything questioning the hope of rain.

1889—Johnstown Flood

June 1   **WILD TURKEY**

Rain at last in the night; freshness fills the air. Scents are released—a good morning for snuffling. Far distant from yesterday. A dogless venture up the new gravelled roadway, from a subdivision to the manipulated farmstead. This course was meant to access housing zoned out in the 90s. Now it's in play again, as a fierce private property: no trespassing wire, uphill all the way, all roadside vegetation sheared, more POSTED at the top, but there's one redemption in this story. Returning downhill on the trail, wild turkey chicks scurry from underfoot, the hen squawks and veers, "toc!" "toc!," to lead the predator away from them. The predator does not seek to predate, swiftly passes on. Hopefully hen and chicks will reunite,

Sinking Creek Journal

but this morning collies' walk is curtailed to avoid what might be a fatal encounter.

*"'What's it for?' I asked again . . .
'Go call a turkey,' he said and left me sitting on a stump, searching for a motion that would make it say 'Eow!' Years later . . . I saw the image of Corbett's handmade box advertised for sale. The Original Cedar-Box Turkey Call, it said. I still have the one Corbett made. It is the original."* Joe Truett, **Circling Back: Chronicle of a Texas River Valley** *(1996)*

June 2　　　　　　　　**Carbonated**

Second rain. Fritillaries on the butterfly weed. Blackberries green but growing. Flying ants in a rock-nest, half hatched, discovered, recovered. Brazilian verbena blooming hither and yon, purple clusters on long stems, jet-shaped leaves, in crannies, edgings. No clue how they got there. All day cooking store-bought Greek foods—buying into carbon, edging gardens—furthering civilization; clipping box elder along driveway—but shouldn't all roadways be blocked whenever possible? CO_2 highest per capita in Wyoming; Tennessee is in the middle. At least haul the Greek foodstuffs home on foot? Too slow—the lamb would spoil—too hot, global warming, heatstroke, run over by refrigerated truck. Pie in the Sky. 20 Acres and a Mule . . .

"If we truly want to stabilize the climate, we need to revive the productivity of the natural world. Acre for acre, restoring a wetland takes more carbon out of the atmosphere than anything else we know how to do." Carl Pope, *"Not Broiled Yet"* (2008)

June 3　　　　　　　　**Catsplay**

The lawn is high and unmown. Pokeweeds and linden seedlings have great expectations that it will remain that way. Tam Lin is stalking toward the porch, a dead chipmunk between his jaws. Held at the spine, it dangles on each side. He looks like he has the mumps. Sets it down in the lawn and curls up: Wait!—it's not dead, it hobbles and writhes toward the brush cover. The cat leaps up, mouths it, carries it back, releases it again. It writhes again, an awkward brown squiggle. He bats it back and forth. He is in his element, elemental. A viewer of the porch can't stand to watch any more, but the viewer sure enjoyed his lamb casserole last night.

1992—Rio de Janeiro Earth Summit begins

June 4   **BORAGE**

Walking today, borage in Ginger's kitchen garden, last year nearly extinguished by mint, now flourishes, spreads and sprawls its hairy limbs, new sprouts, its blue star eyes wide. Borage has a rich historical and present life as flavoring and medication. *Gerard's Herbal* says it will "exhilarate and make the mind glad." Further treading, not softly, toward the wilder side, pool trout have grown longer and the prayer is for promised rain tonight to maintain their habitat. Upslope appears another blue-purple flower, isolated cluster on a short stem, woods bluet (*houstonia purpurea*). Further on, bear evidence: rotted-out pine stump has been torn into for grubs. The farmstead "pond" still bare save that now orange plastic tape outlines two contiguous rectangles overlooking it, suggest a human plan: platform? Bath-house? Gazebo? If so its future inhabitants may have to share it with the black bears; around the pool the hardened ex-mud has preserved, 'till next rain, their massive clawed pawprints.

1892—John Muir founds the Sierra Club

June 5   **SNAKE AND CHUCK**

At least recent rains have kept the creek livable for its inhabitants. At the pool, minnows circulate, and the southern water snake slurps down under an overhang. These snakes are almost part of the human family; they've slithered across the patio, basked with their young on the riprap, have even been spied romantically enlaced on the footbridge that crosses the Nameless Stream. Because the adults in the Southeast are banded, they are often mistaken for copperheads, or, in appropriate regions, water moccasins, and pointlessly executed. Now low wind whips dark clouds and white pine seeds become a brown rain. Branna barks at the pines but not at the seeds—not the pines, it proves, but a clearly juvenile woodchuck about ten feet up in them at an angle of repose across two limbs. Tam Lin is grooming and writhing on a chair below, unaware of this creature, possibly the one in whose defense he was almost killed. Where do the woodchucks live now? They're seemingly done with childbearing, so apparently don't interest Tammy. This woodchuck has black-clawed feet, a triangular nose, sleepy yet observant eyes. Now he or she walks a limb to the neighbors' side. Low sun hits its glowing shape. Suddenly it is gone.

United Nations World Environmental Day

June 6   **RECLAMATION**

"Reclaiming" an abandoned terraced garden. The spading fork descends, thrusts, lifts; no doubt representatives of fifty plant species will have been deracinated once the heroic task is done. Lifting, hurling, uprooting, ruminating that pernicious word *reclamation*. It says "This belongs to us. You took it away. We're getting it back." Thus the Bureau of Reclamation, cultural myth agency, and myth of civilization: irrigating desert "reclaims" it. Does the myth of civilization have Edenic roots? The world first a paradise of green? Now it needs reclamation from the reclaimers. And so it is in this little abandoned garden. Before it was claimed by the humans a few years ago, the "weeds" owned it. They would perhaps argue that their own reclamation project had been interfered with in process by the humans. And one more consideration: the blue fleabane and big babyfaced daisies are too "pretty" to uproot. This is a shameful exception made by the reclaimer. The only authentic botanical beauty contests are those of flowering plants vying for the votes of pollinators. The human exception leads to guilt, a tyrannical eugenics imposed on nature's nonjudgmental diversity.

1932—The Revenue Act of 1932 creates the first national gas tax

June 7   **KINGFISHER**

Roadside: vetch, chicory, clover flourish, blue to purple. Calendula, leek, dill, some basil have grown enough in their nursery pots to be transplanted. Down by the creek, a pause in mowing . . . super-fast dry "kuk-kuk-kuk-kuk," manic bird circling the waterways. The kingfisher is back. Not *the* kingfisher, but after years of absence a presumed descendent. After Sinking Creek was engineered to reduce its periodic flooding, many streamdwellers moved to wetter pastures. The kingfisher's flashing blue used to kuk-kuk up and downstream between long pauses spent on overhanging limbs to plunge for minnows. Green herons, too, hung out on the tulip poplar, sycamore, and linden branches, hunched like monks, waiting to dive. Ironically, even in this teeny microcosm human manipulation for human benefit has devalued habitat for other species. Will the kingfisher appear again? Will it become a summer resident? Stay tuned.

> ". . . *a kingfisher's burnished plunge, the color*
> *of felicity afire, came glancing like an arrow*
> *through landscapes of untended memory."*
>   Amy Clampitt, "The Kingfisher"

June 8   **NEW SUMMER GENERATION**

A chipmunk scoots under Ginger's chair, into the shade garden's wide-leaved shelter. Branna, 90 pounds, rises to investigate. The chipmunk thinks "stupid me," and scoots back under the chair again toward inchoate borderlands. It's very hot, thunderstorms expected. The calendula, leeks, and dill have been planted. A new summer generation waits in the wings or begins to emerge—bunch-petaled white snakeroot all over the slopes, arrival of the (ironically named) black cohosh beside the dump, tall white torch uplifted but flowers nubbed, not yet deployed. The same is true of the New Jersey tea, a band of near-shrubs fronting forest cover where also milkweed heads hang, ready to unfold. And before the New Jersey tea, black raspberries have reddened, the stage before becoming fully "black" and subject to bird pillage. Front yard, the frightening wide-leaved volunteer mullein seems prepared at last to release its yellow flower spike upward, a debt it owes for taking up so much garden space. But debt isn't a strong presence in the ethic of plants—the only debt they owe is to their own species, paid in survival and successful reproduction.

1906—National Monuments Act

June 9   **LANDLESS HABITAT**

Strawberry Lane—suburban ridge road high above Sinking Creek, its every uncultivated edge is yellowed, browned, poisoned. For what earthly reason? Still, beyond this wreckage are deep rich green hillsides, dark with hardwoods. Spared roadsides still display honeysuckle and elders' white flowerplates, queen-anne's lace, pink vetch, star chickweed. The landscaped houses, larger and wider-porched as the lane proceeds southwestward, are "environment-friendly," treed and bushed, but they are high above or deep below the street level; their own forgotten non-native shrubs and flowers are trekking away into the tangle. A young woman, with two yapping, leashed shih-tzus, jogs past one-way cul-de-sac, back again. Brown thrasher tribe flits around, domestically close. Beyond the road-end wood, the lawn of another house on another subdivision road. The new log house, referred to before, lawnless, scrunched into the hillside, is still unsold. A brochure prices it at $468,500. "Professionally Landscaped." People must be fleeing Strawberry Lane: two other 1980's homes have brochures dangling in front. Reduced! $309,900; $319,900. Where does this money come from? Is it all theoretical? What sort of landless habitat, even with a stone fireplace, kitchen island, jacuzzi, could possibly be worth so much?

"*Camus said that certain cities . . . exorcised the landscape. We have a way of life that ostracizes the land.*" Barry Lopez, **The Rediscovery of North America** (1990)

June 10   **STONECROP**

The red-railinged driveway bridge over Sinking Creek is cement-covered railroad rails, the driveway well-gulched by erosive overflow. *Sedum acre*, gold moss stonecrop, lines each edge. The stonecrop was not planted, it volunteered for this unsavory habitat. Tiny succulent leaves underbed lovely petal-point yellow flowers. Once an attempt was made to transplant and garden-train it. Immediate death followed. Like nasturtia, apparently, gold moss stonecrop doesn't want to be moved, especially to rich, fertile soil. *Sedum acre* is populist, proletarian through and through. It has wierd uses—corn removal, boil heading, anus soothing. Despite its bad rep as invasive, the stonecrop on the red-railinged bridge seems to know its place. One can only fantasize it invading inward, covering the concrete, so that one enters the magic land on a golden carpet.

"*Fetch stonecrop mixt with cedar and branches of lilac. . .*"
Walt Whitman, "Song of Myself"

June 11   C OBWEB'S G ARDEN

At last clearing our garden of origin, the first one constructed. It replaced the former owner's rusted metal doghouse, full of bullet holes. Deconstructing the former owner's constructions always involved the risk of tetanus. His pigpen was a labyrinth for infection until a merciful flood swept it away. Here, at the start, full sun hit this eastward slope, and generations of our herbs lived and died there. Imperceptibly a ceiling of green spread, apple, sycamore, jealous for light. There seems to be a critical period when full-sun plants realize they're doomed, the ceiling of green will be permanent. There were still chocolate mint, spearmint, peppermint galore in the summer of 2004 when the massive, gentle border collie, Cobweb, age 15, died, and since he was always a nurturer, he was buried beneath them in this very plot. Now only light-toothed mountain mint, dark green groundcover creeping jenny, and some tall imposing motherwort thrive, the latter showing vivid tiny axil flowers. The project is pruning, restoring sunlight to Cobweb's garden, filling it with as many pungent mints as possible.

"*I would mow the wild grass and horseweeds and long-legged nettles and elderberries, and chop down the tree sprouts, and trim obstructive branches off the nearby trees. It would be hard to describe the satisfaction this opening up would give me.*" Wendell Berry, **The Long-Legged House** (1965)

Sinking Creek Journal

June 12   **WILD LEEKS**

    Looks like the leeks, flat-germinated, were planted too soon among the other alia. In this heat, many of their fine green threads have shriveled, despite repeated watering and tall garlic's shade. Those that survive will need to be rebanked with soil as they grow, to produce the maximum white bulb and tender green stalk. Never will they reach the grandiosity of the supermarket leek, two-thirds of whose weight is destined for compost. Ironically the leek, ridiculed by Shakespeare, and its hillbilly cousin, the ramp, have moved up the food esteem chain in the U.S. Just across the lawn, in one of our ungroomed borderlands, their native wild cousins are thriving; amid diverse "weeds" the wild leeks rise above the crowd, long thin stalks topped by small orbs. Shedding their glassine coverings, these orbs will become miniature versions of the cultivated leek's (*allium porrum*) much larger techno-global flowerhead. The wild leek (*allium tricoccum*) is supposedly far tastier, though far smaller, than its cultivated relative. Here, they are pretty to observe and recognize, but won't be harvested; like ginseng, they face human depredation.

1992—At Environmental Summit President Bush says the U.S. won't sign treaty protecting endangered species

June 13   **FROGS AND SLUGS**

    Two cloudbursts have revived plant and animal energy. Leaves have become tumescent, Elephant Ears unfurl. Here, in the shade garden, rock paved and lined, amphibians and mollusks react differently to heavy rain. A young frog, dark brown, its skin markings still unarticulated appears, alert, and as poised as a frog can be. It has the lean look of adolescence. The low outer wall of stones bears a Buddha, a univalve shell, a stone dragon. Ecumenically, St. Francis presides over the whole. The frog clambers up on the next rock over from the Buddha. There's not much visual difference between them as it sits there, swift tongue occasionally flicking. It meditates on the Veil. Closer in, slugs have surfaced to escape sodden ground. It's hard to realize how many slugs call your garden home unless by chance they all emerge at once. These slugs are slender and orange, with white eye-tentacles. They might well be reticulate taildroppers (*prophysaon andersoni*) but since there are 30,000 snail and slug species in the U.S., only a slugologist would know for sure. Their congregation lies curled up, or slowly guns along the rock surfaces, undulant. The sensuous slug. There are many ways to destroy slugs, viewed as plant predators: diatomaceous earth, stale beer, raised boards you can overturn in daylight to stomp the congregations on their undersides. But ever since an acquaintance jocularly salted a slug, and we watched its agonized desiccation, slugs in these gardens have been regarded more as secret sharers, like frogs, part of the whole.

1979—Sioux Nation wins 17.5 million settlement in land claim suit over Black Hills expropriation in 1877

June 14   **WHITE**

Every leaf drips now when the taller mammal passes through, and more thunderstorms are on the way. Two new white entities emerge in the wet forest. At the foot of a young and light-cramped sugar maple, a family of indian pipes (*monotropa uniflora*), milky stalks rising straight then dangling a bell-shaped "flower," equally white. The indian pipes are famous for being a chlorophyll-less flowering plant; they can grow in the dark. Strangely, they are akin to lady slippers in being for nourishment parasitic on fungi which are in turn parasitic on tree roots; hence their clustering, as though they have chosen this particular maple as the site for a conference, or a powwow. The other white object is a Maxell golf ball (*bealla golvii*) resting innocently at a union of trails. Whence cameth this violently artificial object into the middle of the forest? Is it a portent? Will its natural habitat be the next incarnation of this one?

"What horror to awake at night
and in the dimness see the light
Time is white
mosquitoes bite
I've spent my life on nothing."
            Lorine Niedecker

Sinking Creek Journal

June 15
Spartanburg, SC **EXTINCTIONS**

 Droplets and mist cover all. On the way here, torn white scarves are rising from coves, as though the Appalachian forests burn with wetness. Now the mist envelops live oaks as low South meets high. Here, the outdoors has come in pictorially, and nature lives/dies in opposing representations of loss. Vivian Stockman's mountaintop removal photographs display in tragic color the West Virginia and Kentucky landscapes strip mining has destroyed, 800 square miles of mountains, 1,000 miles of streams, countless life forms from humans to algae sickened and/or killed. What impacts most here is the destruction of color, where color codes life. Rolling green is reduced to grey rock buttes, precipices, massive artificial moraines. And right next door, Mark Catesby's flagrantly colorful birds, alert with primary vivacity. Catesby's *Natural History of Carolina, Florida, and the Bahama Islands* (1731–43), long before Audubon, made alive to Europeans the winged beings of the New World, a number of which they would eventually annihilate. That's the irony of Catesby's color: his parrot of Carolina, his *palumbia migratorius*, his "largest white billed woodpecker on a willow oak"—forever vanished, like the West Virginia mountains.

*1977—Supreme Court upholds the Endangered
Species Act and stops the Tellico Dam project*

June 16
Saluda, NC **RUSTIC ENCLAVE**

 A mountain cleft, and Interstate 26 whizzing by. No clearcut condos here, roads follow the terrain's undulance. A one-street town: one side a *belle époque* commercial block, the other a railroad cut, although now no trains run. A trading path convergence in early white habitation, it was called Pace's Gap. The trains first chuffed up to crest the gap (2,079 feet) on July 4, 1879, after mortal elevation, a three-mile grade, the steepest commercial one in the U.S. then. The celebrity rich rode the grade to get cool—one of many high-ground Victorian tourist retreats (there were

Fred Waage

once 27 hotels here—where did they wedge them all?)—and to meet other celebrities who rose up to summer with them. Now it's a later generation tourism site—artsy, crafts, grills and B & B's; "Holbert's Bee Supply . . ." Exalted "rustic" enclave, initiated by tourism, reborn by tourism, no lumbering devastation in view. A self-justifying human place in Nature. Incidentally, "Saluda" has nothing to do with health; its the Anglicization of the Cherokee su-lu-we-yu (Corn River)—the Green River now, that flows from the mountains downhill.

1980—Supreme Court rules genetically engineered organisms can be patented

June 17
Valle Crucis, NC   **HIGH VALLEY**

Up through the kudzu-choked highway cuts, abandoned kudzu-swathed barns, blank-eyed farmhouses, flapping laundry-draped porches, burned-out country stores, Shirley's Famous Father's Day Barbecue. Then a narrow sinuous two-lane—oxeye daisies, cohosh, queen Anne's lace, stream-threaded wild fields grown over, willows, a high hidden valley. Here an Episcopal monastery was established before the Civil War where streams meet forming a cross, hence "valle crucis." One thinks only in logged-over terrain would streamcourses have been visible enough to create this ideogram. Frank Mast, pioneer trader, unwittingly created the touristic destination the high valley has become—and the only rural space in the U.S. that is designated a National Historic Area. From the Mast Farm Inn's porch one can listen to the varied agonizing splutter tones as motorcycle troupes squeal by. Further back a farm pond dozes in preternatural heat. Beauteous dragonfly, blue-tipped forewings and hindwings, pauses on reed to reed, newt silently dives and surfaces, sunnies cruise in and out of vision. A ponderous carp shows its black shadow. Baking silence.

1902—Bureau of Reclamation established

June 18
Linville Falls, NC   **TOURISTIC RIVER**

    The road to Linville Falls is paved with good-intentioned tourists, and every second structure is a realtor's office, e.g. "17-Acre Estate, 3 Trout Ponds, 3 Septic Permits." The High Country of North Carolina is both a place unto itself, geographically/culturally, and everyplace, levelled by appetitive humanity and earth-encompassing heat. The trail to Linville Falls is beaten smooth, filled with human conversation, complaints of children, chattering baby carriages on stones. Amish bonnetheads gather, eyes down. Surrounding forest is lush, pink and purple rhododendrons. Linville River is slow, Southern, water-smoothed streamlined boulders, cliff walls, below the desperate convulsive swirl as constrained river corkscrews, disappears from upper view, becomes a pure crystal cascade below. All these little kids brought here—will they bring away any lasting awe or love? Fast-paced woodpecker rattle, bullfrog counterpoints in river shade. These beings, unlike the humans, are already at their destinations.

1941—Colorado Aqueduct opened, providing water to Southern California

June 19
Valle Crucis, NC   **LOOM HOUSE**

    This is the "Loom House" on the Mast Farm homestead. It has known almost 200 years of human habitation. Weathered sign at the entrance reads "A. B. Mast Born in this house July 4th 1827." It must have been hot then too. The original tongue and groove beam walls have long been chinked with concrete. Across the road they grow herbs and vegetables, and rent vintage Porsches for mountain day trips. Facing this porch, a massive white oak bulges up and over all the outbuildings. Inside, a long rifle surmounts the stoned-in fireplace. A disfunctional whirlpool bathtub fills half the space. Originally a main building, it later became Mrs. Mast's loom house. Her quilts hang in the Smithsonian. On the second level you can see where the old timbers end, new walls and roofing accommodate guests. In the 19th century the summer sleeper there would have had to crawl on ticking amid infernal heat. This built environment, richly enduring space, is yet abulge with technological dependence. Would A. B. Mast approve of his birth house's use? If a successful capitalist in heaven, he probably does.

1972—Hurricane Agnes kills 127 (to June 23)

June 20
Valle Crucis, NC   **ANT AGONIST**

Exercise in personification: white Italian restaurant patio, rail. Black ant. Large crumb of Italian oil-soaked bread placed in front of ant. Ant proceeds, stops an inch short, twirls feelers: "What the hell is this?" Eventually moves close enough to touch crumb, twirls about, moves back an inch, crouches in ant Thinker position. "Got to figure this out. Got to UNDERSTAND!" Eventually returns, approaches crumb from each of many sides, each time recoils. Pauses to think some more. Walks away down the rail. Pauses again, retraces steps. Stares at crumb closely in existential agony: too appealing to abandon, to intimidating to remain. Another ant happens by. "Hey, bro', check this out? How d'you figure it?" Ant 2 examines crumb from a distance, circles it several times. Thinks. Looks at ant 1: "Let it go, buddy, it's out of our league," ambles away. And still ant 1 remains, Thinks, moves off, returns, Thinks, moves off again . . .

"There is still the unanswered question of how to produce a citizenship that is really qualified for self-government under today's conditions and that can live life at a higher level than a colony of ants." John Storer, **Man in the Web of Life** (1968)

June 21   **GRASS**

The homestead "pond" stays unfilled, unimproved, still, barren earth-patch on a ridge. There's only one really distinctive non-human change: delicate grass rises on all sides, begins to fur up the pond's lower side "dam." Its delicate blades have pierced this hard-beaten earth. A quote: "grass is the forgiveness of nature." If this is a true claim, it certainly applies to the Bastian farmstead's grass. Grass has a positive affect in human discourse. Even Developers have beautiful lawns. Grass suggests a healing process,

Sinking Creek Journal

almost psychic, the calming of "disturbed" land. Thus grass "replaces" West Virginia mine-stripped mountaintops. But worldwide, grasses can be poisonous, knife-edged, dagger-spined. Cultivated, they have become human sustenance; unmodified, they lead a life of their own, safe from our metaphors.

"I am the Grass
Let me work."
Carl Sandburg, "Grass"

June 22   **PUMPKIN PATCH**

The pumpkin seedlings have grown so large now, three leaves, they need a proper home, but the sunny spaces on the shaded property seem all "taken," and past pumpkin failures can be attributed to lack of sun-hours. Then, too, pumpkin vines sprawl widely; they network, seem to thrive in full fields. What pumpkins want most is other pumpkins (and, of course, bees). But what about the grassovergrown patches where castoff lumber, branches, brush, piles? A spot is chosen, in the early morning dew, hands and knees thrusting, striving against the grasses' tenacity. Leif and Faye love to watch humans work. Sometimes Faye helps dig. Cleared, the new pumpkin patch isn't "seen" by the collies as re-nov-ated space. It's just more comfortable for sprawling.

1969—Cuyahoga River (Ohio) on fire

June 23
Beech
Mountain, NC   **OVERDEVELOPMENT AND RURALITY**

The North Carolina (east) side of this mountain is all ski resort and summer home complex, threading roadmasses, ganglaic cancer on a USFS map, so new it's absent because not yet existent on the topozone USGS map. The teetering luxury supervillas shoulder to shoulder, a forest ghetto—$90,000 a half acre, million a house. The Developers' reach has exceeded their grasp; the slope tops and spills over to the undeveloped

Tennessee-facing side, the road networks become unbuilt, forested earth tracks with optimistic cute inhabited names like Milkweed Lane. Here the rhododendron-choked real-estate map plots are 90 percent vertical conifer and hardwood slopes. Here at the very nexus of overdevelopment and pure rurality son Erick has bought five acres of buildable land. Here loosestrife and phacelia, untouched for decades, line the grass track, the cool thin-air forest piled with leaves, fallen timber, dark, silent, flashes of light, one keyhole valley panorama. Five acres snatched from Floridians. The descent from this height is like a descent through varves of human occupancy, from isolated chalets, through clustered power residences, gated communities, into the vale of heat.

1988—Scientist James Hansen testifies to Congress on global warming

June 24 **RUELLIA**

Thunderstorms loom; at the homestead, grass continues to spread despite the baked-hard earth. A muddy rainwater tray in the excavated pool is already drawing dragonflies. Uptrail midpoint, the year's newest wildflower—ruellia, ovate dark green leaves. The USDA reports 39 ruellia species, subspecies, or varieties. Often cultivated, though and invasive, they pose no threat to the foothills of Buffalo Mountain. Named casually Mexican petunias, they are neither Mexican nor petunias. From their leaf bract rise two purple 5-petaled trumpet flowers, more vivid for their purely green surroundings, the carpeted post-bloom iris leaves. Almost at the stream, but Erick points up, and hidden in plain sight one of the three rhododendrons in full white corsage bloom, gauze balls of white in the cleft-rock shade.

Midsummer (Samhain)

June 25 **SUNNY STORM**

Thunderstorms began yesterday afternoon. The stationary human sees dark grey tongues licking over the lighter occluded sky. But the thunder, although closening, seems to sound in every different direction, a child leaping from one concealment tree to another. Stillness fails, wind waves dash against the pines, tip over, thrash the gardens, part the streamside hardwoods, then recede. In new silence, the rain's impact upstream is first heard, slurring foliage. A crescendo of sound and the pelting touch. What a contrast from yesterday—even more violent winds—the linden fingers writhe, but sun still shines westward between clouds, while eastward over beyond Buffalo Mountain, thunder and purple sky. The storm is moving northeast on the Appalachian spine, and we are now mere borderers.

> "The fire-flies flitting about this evening in the rain; they do not mind the showery evening much; we have often seen them of a rainy night, carrying their little lanterns about much unconcerned, it is only a hard and driving shower that sends them home."
> Susan Fenimore Cooper, **Rural Hours** (1850)

June 26   WET DAWN

Early morning, woods dark and wet. Wood thrush very close, moths flutter to daylight refuge. First sunlight seen filtered orange between elm leaf veins. Hieroglyphic box turtle, surprised, lumbers ahead. Is it the same one we met before, grown, or do many plod this unfrequented sanctuary? New Indian pipe clump, bent white tinged with pink, collies clatter chase over dump, white galax torch, first of many, to judge from the covering crowd. By the time we reach the homestead, heat has begun. Two days' rains have filled the "pool"—slimy crusted mudwater. Collies turn up noses. Dam's eroding mud begins filling in trails. Always those unforeseen consequences.

> "Behind every living thing is a steady, comforting, driving pulse. Behind every dream is a rhythm. Listen. You'll feel it."
> Susan McElroy, **Why Buffalo Dance** (2006)

June 27   SUNFLOWER INGENUITY

The heat is on, leaves wilt as they hang on for shadow. Sunflower heads burst out prematurely. Here Mexican and Italian white sunflowers about large enough to be bedded, but volunteers from their ranks are everywhere—where they grew last year, goldfinch-strewn seeds, under feeder sites, in completely random corners. Large clump, one already yellow, surrounds porcelainberry pole—rank of petaled guards. Sunflowers are most ingenious; completely flattened, they poke up their heads anyway. They bend grotesquely to escape shadow. Many non-native species, perhaps because thick growth bears them up in their native land, collapse here from the weight of their own heavy heads. Supported, they seed gracefully, finches and other thistle birds dance on them all fall.

"Interestingly enough, in my gardens the heads of the giant sunflowers always end up facing the east. I have no explanation for this, but the poet would tell us that the plant is awaiting the return of its god, the sun." Charles B. Heiser, Jr. **The Sunflower** *(1976)*

June 28   **FIREFLIES**

Only Tam Lin wants to join us in back to watch fireflies in their glory. Their hordes rise and fall, against the high black treeline, much more illuminating than the light pollution gilding eastern skies. Often groups blink in unison, others seem to have individuated light intervals and flight patterns. Those airborne are males, seeking to light it up with females in the grass below, early morning you can sometimes see underfoot females still alight. Some beetles imitate the females' light and digest gullible suitors. Many humans gather and sell them, since cancer research intensely uses their bioluminescent chemicals, luciferin and luciferase. Like animal experimentation, the marketing of fireflies for this purpose has few opponents in Appalachia. Maybe it is amoral nostalgia, the release of the jarred lights remembered from childhood, promethei unbound . . .

1935—Supreme Court approves strip mining of coal in the upper Midwest

June 29   **DEER DANGER**

Deer are coming closer. Faye has routed a doe, flees crossing right in front of two other dogs and one human. Completely assured on bouldered

Sinking Creek Journal

terrain, the doe, stretched, leaps the largest rocks in single bounds, as though instructed by the terrain itself. Faye returns panting, domesticated into pleasure hunting only. On freeways up north, collided deer carcasses appear every half mile. Municipalities hire sharpshooters to cull herds threatening human migration routes. The most dangerous temperate woodland creature to humans is a horned buck. Reforestation and predator decline have relocated the white-tails into the kiddies' sandbox. Later in the day, as we drink wine on the patio and weary collies sprawl about, on the driveway a brown figure approaches, pauses behind beebalm only a few yards away—another doe, wide-eyed as a Hollywood starlet, scooping fallen birdseed. We call, fearing disaster (=nature). Doe moves not. Finally collies notice, overbark and charge to cover their inattention. By this time the doe is long gone. But there's no sign these elliptical encounters will diminish.

1906—Congress approves Grand Canyon Game Preserve

June 30   **DOG FIGHT**

Considering the benefits plant and animal domestication has provided the human species, and all the conflicts, small and large, it has created... According to Erick, the Neighbor's weimaraner charged a barking Branna, who sidestepped her, a karate move, gave her a tactical nip, let her crash into a rock across the Nameless Stream. Each dog owner blames the other while professing a desire to resolve the issue in a "neighborly" fashion. One might think this a case which could be mediated by that unique human attribute, language. If Branna's owners were themselves dogs, the aggressors humans, the Neighbor (as dog) would have the owners lying on their backs, exposing bellies and throats in submission. Although language does eventually resolve this dispute, kinetics are also involved. The Neighbor (a lawyer) invites Branna's owners onto *his* territory. He parades them through *his* garden, onto *his* spur route connecting to the mountain trail. All as an excuse for them to see the rock where the weimaraner crashed (more accessible from Branna's own land anyway). The result is a verbal negotiation at the crash site, with each party on an opposing side of the Nameless Stream. The Neighbor holds the high ground, and, metonymically, the trail itself, which legally belongs to neither party. Negotiations complete, the Neighbor deigns to cross the bridge to shake hands. This is the kinetic equivalent of war, of quadrupedal sparring. The dogs involved would solve it all more directly.

1885—Division of Forestry established in Agriculture Department

July 1   **WITCH-HAZEL**

Day's end rains have kept the creek running. There's yet no odor of dying stream vegetation. Here, where it bends in the front, its flow doesn't fill its channel, rather it dances purposely among snail-covered rocks. Spiders skitter in the sand, there's an invisible woodpecker overhead. The facing "bluff" brows witch-hazel (*hamamelis viginiana*) bushes, dark green; they bury the stream's flow beneath their looming presence. Later on their seeds will spread, many downstream, which is why it is colonizing the banks there too. Those whose memories go back half a century will recognize witch-hazel's ascerbic scent from the bottles of cure-all, wound-soothing fluid applied by mothers to small boys who never knew its source could be found growing beside the very streams where they gathered tadpoles.

1957—International Geophysical Year begins (through December, 1958)

July 2   **GERMANDER**

Buffalo Mountain seems blue on this cloudy day. Down here, the garden across the stream, there's one purple eggplant swelling, other purple flowers yearning to be fertilized. Beside, amid weed-choked stream border, a colony of pink germander, "wood sage," a spire of buds unfolding upward. Each year this wild swath seems to specialize in a new flower; before, it was the mullein's tall yellow spires, but they did not reseed. This pink germander is not the wall variety so popular in European gardens; rather, each plant is stalwart, freestanding, dark green ovate leaves in alternation. It is a nonfragrant mint, characterized as toxic though listed in many herbals. Behind it, the creek itself seems to be losing its flow. Song sparrows call—their nest is near. Blackberries are steadily blackening. A tree fall-bent elm's leaves are yellowing. Air is thick.

> "How little we know as yet of the life of plants—their hopes and fears, pains and enjoyments!" John Muir, **A Thousand-Mile Walt to the Gulf** (1866; published 1916)

July 3 — HIGH POINT

Midmorning—a plott hound ambles up the road, which seems to vanish into mountain wall but actually curves in continuous concealed break. Climbing Buffalo Mountain's back shoulder... trees close in, higher elevation conifers, further back white rhododendron, then higher, milkweed, reddish-pink joepyeweed. Just about the highest point, a turnoff, portrayed as a road on USFS map, hairpin turning over the source of Sinking Creek, object of this quest. Behold—there is no road, rather a "designated" ATV trail: notice board, fees, regulations, phone numbers of local hospitals! They think of everything. Better one designated route than wandering freedom to tear up the forest floor. At Dry Creek Road's many turnoffs, male humans gather, exchange words, wounds, booze, drugs. Abandoned now, detritus-smeared: dead creekside fires, burned-out auto parts, food containers, shattered bottle rocket remains. And pervasive urine scent through which a clear stream tumbles over mossy rocks.

> "The best people, like the best wines, come from the hills."
> Edward Abbey, **A Voice Crying in the Wilderness** (1989)

July 4 — VALE

Ungroomed creekside trail network crosses, rises round mysterious cliff, descends again. Fallen fences, rich ground cover, Virginia creeper, protective darkness amid day, sycamores spread above, encounter steep slope spruce. Woodscent. When this land was farm pond, the Nameless Stream poured from here straight to Sinking Creek—its dry gully persists, ancient windfalls, abandoned steel-capped cement wellhead. Where more sun strikes, yellow pale touch-me-nots (*impatiens pallida*) already bloom, orchidic flowers coy in their foliage. This trail tangle is right below a neighbor's vehicle station, double-wide, trash yard it would take a tortilla curtain to conceal. Turn your back, though, and it's a fragrant vale.

1845—Thoreau moves to Walden Pond

July 5   **BRANCHING STRATEGIES**

As trees grow through years, plants' light access, in cultivated space, alters subtly. It takes a while to understand this. A plant's location must be chosen in prospect of its long-term light needs and the growth of its neighbors. Thus, the franklinia bends southwest as it slowly matures, since the stream's tree wall has risen to meet, and interfere with, the morning sun. Whereas its relative, the mature and towering cucumber tree, is straight as an arrow, since it was planted, and rose to maturity, when all the neighboring growth was still low. As has often been observed here, treelife wars for sun, and the human cultivator can't necessarily foresee what branching strategies it will employ. Thus the cultivator, to maximize survival, must intervene and if necessary, without killing, counter these strategies. Here the cultivator must extend pruning hook, climb 18-foot ladder, guide hook between power lines, reach sawblade to black walnut branch, endure agony of musculature, sawdust pouring in face until the branch thrashes, toppling, finish off the cut, try to avoid power lines again, pull fallen branch to streamside—all so the introduced exotic, spoiled Japanese cherry can be enlightened again.

"The younger specimens are marvels of symmetry, straight and erect as a plumb-line, their branches in level whorls of five mostly, each branch as exact in its division as a fern frond and thickly covered by leaves, making a rich plush over all the tree . . ." John Muir, **My First Summer in the Sierra** (1911)

July 6   **THICKET**

Blackberry jungle. By now almost half have turned from red to black, reached the point of ripeness where they fall into the hand at a touch. But the touch is likely to accompany a jab of pain. When God cast Satan from heaven he landed on a blackberry bush. Its thicket is an intimidating

Sinking Creek Journal

monoculture, the harvester has to kill to reap. Even reaching complexly past intersecting thorn arcs risks death by a thousand cuts, and the largest, darkest berries seem to hang just beyond the arm's reach. A bear has no such impediments. But there's a certain logic to the tangle as far as humans go. Bears shit in the woods, but blackberry seeds consumed by humans are less likely to end up where they can propagate. So we humans curse the bushes for encroaching on our land, slash them down, yet forage the edges of their impenetrable kingdom, gathering their fruits with a maddening tender dexterity.

"By the Deerfield River in Massachusetts, a dozen years ago, two inebriated bears full of cider lurched all over a nearby road . . . and got up on the hood of a police car. Massachusetts closed its bear season for the duration of the hangover." John McPhee, **Table of Contents** (1985)

July 7 **STILL MOTION**

Small motion—minnows, water striders, black-winged damselflies, turbulence around stones; rusty daddy longlegs scurrying, complex ant colonies, grub societies disturbed, boiling; vibrations—leafstalk recoils, spiders retreating, webs throbbing; companion horseflies following, landing, slapped away; white moths rising, diving for cover; sound waves—distant hammering; gnats in sunbeams, inch-long toad poised; atoms spinning in infinity, all the motions smaller than perception, carbonated, bubbling life. And yet the forest is still.

1958—President Eisenhower signs Alaska Statehood Bill

July 8 **PRUNING #2**

Of all the cultivated plants, the butterfly bushes (*buddleiae*) probably suffered the late April freeze worst. Their branches, already leafed, became plaguey black, images of death. In this case alone the dictate "leave a plant alone to recover" was not heeded. Ginger pruned them ruthlessly and *then* left them alone. But now in July they are green, and the most prosperous one is displaying its purple plumes, visited by innumerable bees, insects, and latecoming butterflies—red admirals, black swallowtails, skippers. One of the gardener's most fulfilling rituals is clipping these bushes' spent plumes so the energy to produce successors is not sapped. Although this clipping is an unnatural act, it seems to express a harmony. In the middle of the bush, arm raised, snipping, a rich, spicy scent surrounds the gardener hooked on branches, looking outward, in fantasy fusion attractive as the bush itself.

"Yearly, the utility companies send out cherry-pickers to hack out the center limbs, the disfigurement being inflicted so wires will not be interfered with, and no one protests this barbarous practice. Yet if it were to be suggested that the same trees be pruned in the European manner, cries of horror would go up." Eleanor Perenyi, **Green Thoughts** (1981)

July 9   **MOLTING**

Arrowheads, tiny fossils, colored stones, dead butterflies, acorn caps, cicada exoskeletons: some contents of a small male human's treasure box in the times when such humans roamed neighborhoods rather than video screens. There've been lots of empty cicadas recently—light brown, perfect in every detail, feather-weight, clinging head up on a vertical surface. The inhabitants have climbed from underground, wriggled out of their wrappings, aspired upwards. Sometimes you can find a whole society of hollow frames in the same position, side by side, like the ghosts of dead airplanes. The casting of this tegument is intriguing, maybe because so alien to human biology, though our wounds scarify and heal over in not so different a process. Imagine us molting similarly, human skins of every age and condition cast by the roadside. One might collect all one's earlier skins as one grew and hang them in a museum of one's self.

1954—Einstein-Russell manifesto against
nuclear weapons development issued

July 10   **COMPANION-FLY**

The syrphid fly is back! Actually, over the years, many generations have passed, but about this time each summer one—usually only one—

goes into action among the scarlet phlox. The syrphid fly (generically "hover fly") looks half bee and half fly. Its body is striped yellow and black, seems fuzzy to the viewer; it moves with hummingbird precision among flowerheads, growing longer and more imposing as summer progresses. Sometimes it hovers, making eye contact, almost acknowledging the human presence. The good deeds of the syrphid fly are those of its larvae—voracious aphid-eaters. The mature fly, personified, becomes somewhat a companion-fly. The human can feel comfortable in its presence, sharing its love of flowers.

1985—Greenpeace ship Rainbow Warrior bombed in New Zealand

July 11   **TIMELY RAINFALL**

Very early morning. Still. Grey obscurity. Mourning doves coo among the witch hazel, screech owl's beating call far back on the mountainside. Then tiny cold droplets prick skin, slowly increase in frequency until they can be heard on skylight cover and seen vibrating every leaf. Cardinals fluff waterproof in snowball bush. Birdbaths slowly fill. First whole day's rain in many weeks. Sycamore tops toss. Linden fingers dance. The topheavy phlox and gladioli bend. Washed of dust and pollen, green surfaces brighten. Pines whip menacingly. Tam Lin and Faye observe through the cat window and, unlike us, hope it will end soon.

United Nations World Population Day

July 12   **WEED GARDEN**

Between driveway and white pine wall is the weed garden—thin strip once drainage channel, it welcomes all who volunteer to grow there. All illegal immigrants allowed. Most populous ethnicity is poison ivy, delighted to climb the fencing that spans the treeline, which it can adorn at will and use to launch its hairy vines up toward tree crowns. Small opportunistic hardwoods thrive here—chinquapin oaks, American elder, box elder. There's much ghettoization. Bull thistles stick together as do gangly redstemmed pokeberries. Where more light falls, jewelweed gathers, even this early some of its orange blossoms under leaves. A couple of years ago red raspberries emerged here as from nowhere, multiplied, were trellised, but April frost hit them hard and now only a few round reddening clumps, overmastered by other vines. Only pulled up is the ragweed, victim of all too human personificatory dislike. Every ego garden needs an id, it seems, as outlet, contrast and acceptance that human choice for cultivation are arbitrary.

1892—*Frederick Jackson Turner's famous lecture
proclaims the closing of the frontier*

July 13   **WILD DOMESTICS**

This morning a doe in the front yard listens with only mild curiosity to dogbark, lingers, paces through trees, pauses in the driveway so the driver has to beep her off, eases to streamside, her protected freeway. She evokes the days before annexation, when domestic animals did their wilding on the property—pigs racing through, cattle browsing flowers, large goose herd hanging out with mallards until finally their upstream owner was located, a netted troop descending like slavecatchers on them in the night. An immense hog inhabited abandoned truck next door. Rural homesteads still fill the valley, but the clamor of nonhuman animals is gone, the semi-wild's silent ranks—deer, raccoons, woodchucks—can hardly replace their predecessors' pungent familiarity.

"*The deer was small, about the size of a whitetail fawn, but
apparently full-grown. It had a rope around its neck and three
feet caught in the rope. Someone said the dogs caught it that
morning and the villagers were going to cook and eat it that night.*"
Annie Dillard, **Teaching a Stone to Talk** (1982)*

July 14   **ON THE RISE**

It seems mushrooms are on the rise: russula (bright red), milky caps, new shelf fungus on old windfalls. Cool morning, collies drink their fill from reliable vacuum canister. Shaved homestead is now about 2/3 revegetated, especially on the side where afternoon sun lights longer. But vegetation is as much pokeweed as grass—some whole patches of it at different developmental stages. Leif immerses himself in the "pond," immediately becomes brown collie. On home ground, broad arrogant hibiscus blooms unfold, stella d'oro lilies considered done in by frost form late buds, light purple thyme flower cascade, Japanese eggplants fingernail moons, swelling . . .

> "Rain, and then the cool pursed
> lips of the wind draw them
> out of the ground . . ."
> Mary Oliver, "Mushrooms"

July 15   GARLIC GLEANING

Time to harvest garlic. Its stems have bent over, covering the allium garden, and either browned at the top or begun to display their spherical flowers. Since they're all among chives and leeks, a trowel has to loosen them delicately, they need to be lifted out with as little soil disturbance as possible. Some bulbs are plump, with multiple cloves, some never got going, just a single one. Roots bearding bulb are twisted off, clipped with scissors, rubbed softly to remove soil and cellophane outer skin. There must be at least a hundred bulbs. There's a professional braiding technique for garlic, but it would take the rest of the summer to perform it, so most will be just roped and hung, others divided and replanted for a November harvest.

1885—Niagara Falls Reservation opens as a state park

July 16   BEAR MAN

Our friend Dave, a super-gourmet cook, has come over to pick blackberries. He'll surely lose some weight in his special thorn-resistant top-to-toe coverall. He picks up his blue pail, plunges into the thicket exultantly, Faye beside him to help out. Dave has a large frame, and, half-visible, thrashing, exclaiming with glee, he resembles a big bear or a big little boy. It's mammalian and primal. Apparently the berries are thick in there. The timid merely observe him and the new unheralded wildflowers at their border. One is bergamot, tousled thin-petaled heads bent on long swaying stems, relatives of bee balm, rich in medicinal properties. Right next door, on similar stems, the more spectacular golden tickseed: violent gold petals surrounding blood-scarlet head, you can see them from far away, glaring . . .

1945—First atomic bomb detonated at Alamagordo test site

July 17   **COMINGS AND GOINGS**

Cooling and intermittent rains have brought freshness to the creatures of nature. Washed leaves transpire, spread. Dragonflies dance over replenished pools. Pumpkin leaves, still unblighted, cover their patch, even begin to utter tendrils and buds. Streamside jewelweed has taken over, to watch ripples parade and await the right late blooming time. Every bed and container seems to support at least one volunteer sunflower. But now also the beebalm is passing its prime, reluctant to concede its new territories to insidious powdery mildew. The cucumber tree's peanut-shaped seeds, fallen on inhospitable ground, whiten and decay. For every two steps forward, two steps back.

1916—Federal Farm Loan Act establishes a land bank for farmers

July 18   **OPEN HOUSE #2**

Around the house now one finds stag beetles on their backs, feet waving in the air. Some have already passed. Why are they indoors, upended? Are they light-drawn as so many other creatures? A lit open house at night is really a great trap, particularly, but not exclusively, for winged creatures. How much penance can one do in an open house? How many moths' brief lives briefly save lifted back over the sill, wings already clumsy-finger-damaged? The spider seems content under the toilet or webbed around the smoke alarm. Bedroom firefly flash deters sleep, houseflies explode from houseplant egg-caches. The wasps are most frequently rescued, to mutual benefit. The best tool for open house wasp rescue is plastic food container with lid: swift close, angry buzz, wide release. The wasp deserves respect, release from confinement, but forget any gestures of gratitude. The wasp is Itself and flies alone.

*1976—First diagnosis of Lyme Disease**

July 19   **FULL**

Complete summer pattern—full heat, afternoon shower, through it all, hounds' constant baying, hammering on wood; then at night constant wavelike cricketing. Robert Frost, or rather his ovenbird, says midsummer is to spring as one to ten, and the rising of the cricket churn bears that truth out, querying as the ovenbird does what to make of a diminished thing, answering by overcompensation. Yet the illusion of a static prime resides in the full-circle red-rimmed gerbera daisy against blue lavender. The daisy speaks no diminution, a sun fixed at noon, whereas constantly the crickets crick of constant change.

1869—John Muir begins writing **My First Summer in the Sierra**

July 20   **SILENT FOREST**

Seems like three hickory types on the steep slope are already sending their seeds groundward, littered together, enmingled like the trees themselves—pignut (brown husk), bitternut (thin green), shagbark (fat, eggshaped) . . . nourishment, eventually, for many other creatures and the Earth itself. New mushroom varieties in coy black fungus colonies, nut-rounded dark spheres on dead wood and hygrophori, nested cheek to ruddy cheek beside an intermittent stream. Forest very silent today—flashes of clear sunlight, distant thunder, coal car rumble. Turkeys baited again: spilled corn jug. Down by Sinking Creek the jewelweed is really beginning to flower now—orange flamelets like the first burst of popcorn. Butterflies flit, soon will have all the jewelweed covered. Three hot collies flop in the Nameless Stream, letting it flow through and into them, big hairy leeches.

Fred Waage

"The forests of America brought out in us, as fate will do, both our best and worst; they molded and they exposed us." Donald Culross Peattie, **A Natural History of Trees** (1948)

July 21   **THRESHOLD**

Almost chilly July morning, the boughs are filled with mist. It's dark at nine o'clock back here under the hemlocks, by the great fallen spruce root earthwall. The Nameless Stream curls shallowly around stones and windfall, steep rise, rockface indentation, massive beech trunk. From the former waterworks a mysterious black pipe, cement pillar—abandoned city. Green Darkness Kingdom, no sightlines out, its mood enters the intruder, lowers the pulse, slows the feet. One could curl and repose, millenially content, slowly soothed by moss. But the companion dogs will have none of it; they're uncomfortable without lucidity. Burst forth into sun as over an allegorical threshold between worlds. Glancing back, no sign of an entrance to the dark world, just sycamore curtain, trailing black raspberry vines; ahead, daylight and the homely house.

"The pileated woodpecker, materializing from thin air; the bobcat, startled, vanishing back into it. The red cedar hammered into bar rock; the arctic tern hurtling 12,000 miles from pole to pole; duckweed rising from wintering muck to bloom in the pastures of light. These are deeds of a separate world. We have taken ourselves from that world." David Brendan Hopes, **A Sense of the Morning** (1988)

July 22   **FUNGI**

Record low last night. Nonhumans and humans seem relieved. Neighbors' nest remodelers hammer and scrape energetically, even on Sunday. The dawning woodland flower is southern agrimony, a yellow-budded shaft rising from triplicate toothed leaves, like an underachieving goldenrod. Decaying forest wood—aged windfalls, outrutted stumps—has become a fungal dormitory. Nestled in fibrous conifer stump detritus, pear-shaped puffballs, brown, spherical; shelf fungi—turkey tails, grey-brown, symmetrically curvolinear, in perfect descending order; squamous polypore,

Sinking Creek Journal

bright orange, just starting out at a trunk's cut end. Thick sycamore limbs line the semi-abandoned garden down by the bog, where every day a gelid milk-white, imposingly pure shelf fungus, variety unknown (there are at least 500 species) spreads along them, creates discordant smoothness in rough-textured space. One other entity, nonfungal, has also just made its appearance, sprawling out from roadside brush: the bright orange trumpet creeper, proclaiming July.

> " . . . I saw at the root of a small shrub, a singular and beautiful appearance, which I remember to have instantly apprehended to be a large kind of Fungus which we call Jews ears, when, at that instant, my father being near, cried out, a rattlesnake, my son, and jerked me back . . ." William Bartram, **Travels** (1791)

July 23   **FEEDER SOCIOLOGY**

Bird feeder sociology—species interaction around a food source, human-imposed and centralized. First, the tolerance and rivalry of ground feeders (e.g. jays, mourning doves, sparrows). Doves jump jays, jays bounce away, despite their initial arrogant demeanor. Power in number. Doves descend as vocal group, moil about, leave in group, perch on wires in group. Hairy woodpeckers, nuthatches, less obtrusive, often in couples, divide their time between trunk bugs and easy sunflower fare. Cardinals, magisterial above the fray, spoon. Increasingly goldfinches teeter on sunflowers upside down: "hurry up and ripen your seeds." Wrens, perky, fast moving sparks, tip tails-up. It's like Hardees—they arrive in rushes. Later in the afternoon it's the grey squirrels, sharp black eyes, indignant tails, leaps to longsuffering magnolia branches, hanging gymnastically, heads down, over feeders, pre-empt the birds. Sometimes, Branna, bored, charges them. Squirrels flee, birds return.

1972—ERTS-1, first earth resources observation satellite, launched

July 24   **UNBUILT**

There's "progress" transforming the former Native American cornfield site into condos. Blue port-a-john, soil bared, irregularly wounded, dismally mudpooled after rain. White van back in the field: operations center? Rusted earth-moving machinery in dull repose. Erick visited "his" former site last month—it was already so overdug no flints could be found. White mallows still cling to the brushy road edge. Otherwise, it is a study in stasis—undone, unbuilt. Facing mountain slope blue, brown gashes, green grasses. Pre-habitation is usually destructive—lands lying preorganized for human convenience, increate yet. And the world over, bustling bipeds tangled in this process of creating a new topography.

1934—Dust Bowl heat wave hits its peak (Chicago 109°)

July 25   **MOVING OUT**

Across the street from the Praise and Truth United Pentecostal Church are Nappy's Bar, and, further down, Bill Joe Bob's Bar and Grille. Further out are Iron Street and Steel Street—only the names survive that old dream of a Southern Pittsburgh. The Snap-On Tools factory is for sale; the used goods store is called God's Corner. Slowly flower-wreathed company town style houses float off in space, the shallow valley opens out into groved pasture. Queen Anne's lace, blue chickory, red clover, wild peas and other vetches pattern the fields with such a regularity of color grouping one might think them in a patterned fabric. Under sun they glow, seemingly untouched, the cool dappled brown treeshaded cattle are scarcely visible. Land rises, jolts down—St. John Milling Company, one of the oldest working mills in Tennessee, seems dusted entirely with brown powder. Watauga River just beyond is milky green after rain, a solitary wadered fisherman, the tiny town of Watauga curve-nestled, permanently sleepy, its every street a dead end.

1963—limited Nuclear Test Ban Treaty signed

July 26   **GLOAMING**

The old bird friend back again, green heron (*butorides virescens*), compact hunched body, brown and white striped neck, iridescent aqua-green wings and body (hence *virescens*). When tree cover was lower,

Sinking Creek Journal

several might peer from sycamore branches right above creek, white eyes focused for frogs or minnows. The green heron is no bigger than a crow, and today's was initially mistaken for one, hopping on twigs, but its unique color pattern gave crow the lie. A cautious species, the green herons of Sinking Creek seemed nonetheless to feel secure poising for prey, even close to the house. Did low water flow and less prey drive them away? Is this but a casual visit?

Gloaming, deep summer. Far off dogs and machines. A late female ruby throat tests the purple verbena. Weighty mourning dove collective descends, pecks, disperses, reforms, descends. Close cicada rehearses August chant. Insects hover about overweight red and white phlox heads. The green wall darkens, first low down, creeping upward, while the cross valley hill is still misty blue-green. Ki wanders over for a tail-pull, he's matted as usual from long periods coursing under bushes. Heavy hibiscus flowers, pink extravaganza, buds in good supply, but spread and wilt fast. The mullein's yellow button tip remains, a dot of permanence.

"When we looked out from under the tent, the trees were seen dimly through the mist, and a cool dew hung on the grass, which seemed to rejoice in the night and with the damp air we inhaled a solid fragrance." Henry David Thoreau, **A Week on the Concord and Merrimack Rivers** (1849)

July 27   Wet and Wild

Grey, somber morning in the wet wild field. *Copia*—every space is taken, boneset and other vines unite the tall plants, milkweed is growing pods, head-high ironweed preparing flowers, and the carpeted thick grasses and alder seedlings. A celeriac scent fills the field air, a blizzard-felled sycamore, still rooted, bisects it, young trees have sprung and grown from its living corpse, opportunistic acanthus bows over them. The trunk forms a mini-habitat of higher growth, makes a tongue of underwood darkness spread out into the field. Southward now the field is higher and drier, early goldenrod, not bushed-out and showy but slender, long thin steeply-grooved leaves, beside the first wingstem, resembles a sunflower with confused petals. Soon wingstem will bloom widely, especially along the creek, many lanterns of already aging sun . . .

"It is interesting to watch this retaking of old ground by the wild plants, banished by human use . . . many old habitués of the field have come back to their old haunts. The willow and brown birch, long ago cut off by the Indians for wattles, have come back to the streamside, slender and virginal in their spring greenness. . ." Mary Austin, **The Land of Little Rain** (1903)

July 28 — BREAKOUT

Droplets cover the massive thread-leaved dog fennel, make of it a Christmas tree in July. Scattered half-inch green grasshoppers on wet brush, wasp aroused, desultory bumblebee at the horse nettles. Every step flushes up moths. Overnight the sea mallow from Monticello has begun pinkly flowering, although its proper habitat is marshland. Maybe continual moist weather has inspired it, stems so long they have to be tied, baby mallows scattered beneath. Above the mallow, song sparrow perched on dead snowball bush branch breaks out, full-voiced. You can see its whole dishevelled body convulse, head bob with effort, to emit notes so much larger than it is.

1977—Trans-Alaska Pipeline goes into full operation

July 29 — UNIVERSE OF CROW

A most bizarre incident while driving. Crows frequent Sinking Creek Road regularly—there's always a supply of roadkill or litter to peck at. Unlike the turtles, whose misplaced faith allows them to cross the road slowly, or the dashing squirrels of folly, or the possums who seek eternity as speed bumps, the crows are savvy to vehicles and always hop to the roadside. A driver comes to assume they will take care of themselves. This afternoon, exception proves rule: one crow hops too slowly, crashes right between the vehicle's eyes, bounces off the windshield onto the roof. For a microsecond there, against the view, is seems much larger than life, as though the driver's entire vision is blanked black wings and yellow legs: a universe of crow, "flying the black flag of himself." Stop, peer backward,

Sinking Creek Journal

check roof, no crow, nor driving back later. An omen, the companion suggests, a bad omen, crow as symbol of death. Crow killed? Death, thou shalt die.

"Why would anyone dream about ravens?"
Bernd Heinrich, **Mind of the Raven** (1999)

July 30   CONDOVILLE

This stretch of road is almost wild, winding as it rises past the power line cut. There's a Civil War-era 20-chimneyed brick mansion with barn and brown-white goats, a steep wooded dropoff to irregular streambed, opening glimpses of overrun farmland. Blooming honeysuckle tangles the view. One would scarcely know we are in condoville until the road opens out, old farms, one sold for a strip condo, abandoned barns, boarded-up farmhouses, finally the public school. So much open land has been subdivided, one can scarcely believe that in its first incarnation Cherokee School was a barren wooden cube amid cropland. Now it has companions with brick mailbox frames surrounded by cute flowers. An elderly farm couple lived in their sagging house across the road in the "old" 1980s; their reduced holding was full of animals, field-trips crossed to pet cows and sheep. They and their house have died, all their land subjected to the iron gates of death.

"This was the soft underbelly of the last great wilderness on the continent. I could see the civilization to the south lying against it like a hungry young animal, probing, pushing, exploring, milking the untouched resources above, and as it fed, making its growth felt." Sigurd Olson, **The Lonely Land** (1961)

July 31   DREAM OF ROOTS

White full moon sets through mist at sunrise. Mist powers against mountains, hangs condensed from spiderwebs, hovers over noisy, satisfied creek opaqued by ravaged detritus of drought. Leaves are limp with its weight. It's like the weeklong rain's reluctant departing ghost. Now the valley lacks clarity. In a dream of roots we are grounded, but our permanence is ephemeral, our foliage can all wither in a season. The moon is a ghost, misty trees are ghosts, the white miterwort tapers, the white destroying angels in hell-green tree moss. Such is the mind's romance till first red sunglow bears down on it like a firetruck out of control.

"... all nature is linked together by invisible bonds, and every organic creature, however low, however feeble, however dependent, is necessary to the well-being of some other among the myriad forms of life with which the Creator has peopled the earth." George Perkins Marsh, **Man and Nature: or, the Earth as Modified by Human Action** (1869)

August 1   **HEALING LANDSCAPE**

For a very long time this low swale held a working farm, wedged between rail tracks and beer distributors on one side, Doozy trucktops on the other, the interstate at its base—brick farmhouse, stately barn, cattle and horses on pasture grazed green. A perfect fit of geography and use. The house, abandoned, went first, then the barn, the stock, the very earth surface, recreated as massive supermarket, paved lot, gas pumps. What remains, several years after this (con)struction are paradoxically preserved wild fields, overgrown humps of bulldozed land, a once-stripped stream now readorning itself with baby sycamores and reed grass. Look behind the Big Box and spread are acres and acres of the pastureland gone to seed, free and hidden, all the way to the base of Buffalo Mountain . . . colonies of daisy, fleabane, red clover, steaming in the heat, brown Johnson grass, white mallow at the damp edges. The supermarket is a shield—at least for now. In view a terminus, actually just a point, a blip, a caravanserai dropped on a healing landscape.

1946—McMahan Act creates the Atomic Energy Commission

August 2   **BOILING HOT**

It's boiling. The pumpkin leaves wilt, the houseplants left outside to water get sunburnt. Tropical exotics thrive. Elephant ears balloon. Brazilian

Sinking Creek Journal

verbena—the long stems with ultra-thin leave and vibrant purple flowerheads—continue to spring up and expand; the allium garden ones shoulder out the sage. Black swallowtail, blue skipper, scarlet-thoraxed dragonfly attack at once a single verbena bloom. Its nectar seems an upper to insects: yellow jackets become more frenetic and potentially hostile. Some would think August the truly cruellest month, but not the tropical and ornamental plants, rose of sharon, jacaranda. This is for them a time to strut. However, August is not kind to border collies, even those with tuxedo cuts—and other furry mammals. The collies pretend they're frustrated by inactivity, but when their owners, at their command, brave the hot lawn chairs outdoors, they unobtrusively slink back in to lie on top of air conditioning vents.

> "The corn was high, and the long blades glistened in the sun. The harvest was all around him, and the tassels were dark and damp with the rain and the great green ears were heavy and full of fragrance."
> M. Scott Momaday, **House Made of Dawn** (1968)

August 3   **HEAVY HEADS**

Sunflowers—their first bloomers anyway—have begun to lose their petals and turn all seed. By this time their heads are so heavy many need props or they'll fall to earth and rot out. The goldfinches are increasingly interested in them, practicing upside down poses as the seeds ripen. Where there are birds and sunflower seed, the yellow ones are the universal volunteers. The Mexican sunflowers, spoiled hand-raised cousins, still have a long way to go. All the feeder birds' favorite observation point is the ancient freeze-ravaged snowball bush. Goldfinches observe sunflowers from her, cardinals and chickadees eye the feeders, ruby-throated hummingbirds suck beebalm below her; further back the brown deer flanks can be spied—grazing prematurely fallen apples.

1492—Columbus sets out for the New World

August 4   **MYCOPHILIA**

Mycophile paradise, August and later: napkin amanita—slightly pointed cap, poison-aura green; caesar's mushroom—striking tall stem, orange-red cap; dingy tricholoma—camouflaged, color of the duff from which it rises; salmon entoloma—orange in the occasional streambed; coral fungi—white and orange, thready, intertwining; "pig's ears" (*gomphus clavatus*)—just one ear here, purple, deep ferruled cup, suitable for poisoning Hamlet's mother, or, bitten, changing Alice's height, at every elevation among all these agrimony's yellow wands. Up top, the "pond" is more sickly green than ever, white-dotted, nearby an empty bag "Producer's Pride Whole Corn;" from dogsniff body language one gathers the turkey shooters still lurk around like afternoon thunderstorms.

1977—Department of Energy created

August 5   **MONARCHS AND VIRGINS**

The monarch seems to be searching the right egg-laying milkweed, cruising and, as it were, "sniffing," each one in turn. Of course, since she lays only one egg on each plant, it can't really be a matter of choosing the "best" plant: maybe she's preselecting a whole list—there are so many in this grove, most still upright with bulging pods—and filing it in her butterfly brain. Maybe it is the whole grove of plants that's being appraised—for location? Safety? Proximity to others? Good school system? In any case, it takes about four days for a monarch egg to hatch, so the milkweed grove should be revisited to judge between anthropocentric speculation and reality. Twined through and around these milkweeds, ironweeds, tiny virgins-bower blooms are opening. Their low vines are so entwined, so loaded with buds, they will soon appear almost one white sheet of color (hence "bower"). Downhill, the old abandoned telephone pole has for years been home of Virginia creeper, so thickly wound up and down it, the pole itself is hardly visible. These creeper vines are more advanced than others on the property—their green has partially bronzed, but the berry clusters hanging down from them are still green. At the foot of the pole a family of wild hyacinths has established itself, elongated purple clustered stems bending out toward the sun.

Sinking Creek Journal

1963—the U.S., U.K. and Soviet Union sign the nuclear test ban treaty

August 6   **BURNING**

    Red sun over the supermarket, a perfect circle. Warm mist fills the tree-swallowed city, a scent like camera film from the Eastman plant in Kingsport, though no one uses film any more. The human community begins to stir, pumping exhaust into the mix. The big rigs cruise over from North Carolina. They will eat you alive. The factories have died. Rusted earth movers on concrete slabs. The sun's face now has cloud scabs. We are burning up at dawn.

1945—Hiroshima bombed

August 7   **NEGOTIATING LIGHT**

    Lying on the ground, looking up a tree's trunk from its base, you can see, invent, or infer its history of growth. Then you, the human, can, like a parasite, attach this history to your own world of consciousness. This white pine, for example, was a living Christmas tree in 1980, burlaped roots, tall as an average person. After Christmas it was planted beside the house. Like Leif, who weighs ninety pounds but remains, in his own mind, a forever puppy, the perceptual Christmas tree was for a while a perpetually person-high Christmas tree. The next summer it almost died, bearing bagworm nests like ornaments, but then it grew, imperceptibly at first, negotiating for light between the house on one side and the row of taller pines, also growing, on the other. In this negotiation it slanted its growth, the early years, away from the house wall, but when it was house-high, a turn the other way purchased more light, since, alas, the house was not getting taller. The observing eye today can trace in its slanted growth pillar the history of these decisions. The children the tree entranced in youth have themselves reached their maximum height and, mobile, left to follow their own light. The tree, tall now, intrudes heavy limbs over gardens and denies them sun. Its pruner will celebrate its will to survival, and the memories it, presumably unknowing, calls forth.

Fred Waage

1978—*President Carter declares Love Canal a disaster area*

August 8   **HEAT AND SURVIVAL**

All over the eastern U.S. hot metal blazes and shimmers. No clouds. Here, among great trees, we are cooler, but still in a state of danger. This stream-swollen space can support the wild ones, they can burrow and sip the everflowing Nameless Stream. Winged creatures here have not modified their behavior: hummingbirds and bees course the wiltless butterfly bush. In climatic extremes the humans and dependent domestics are still more vulnerable, more than six degrees separated from simple survival. How much heat, how high, how long, would begin to crumble these layered towers of support, and eventually cast us, alone, living or dead, upon a blazing earth?

"Whether or not it is too late to hold global temperatures below the critical threshold, it is clear that the greater the cuts we make, the lesser the eventual impact will be." George Monbiot, **Heat** (2007)

August 9   **WEB**

Immune to heat and asymmetry, the spider spins an afternoon web between trellissed ivy and ligularia. Much too small to be an orb-weaver, she also has a different style. Her matrix is a vertical-horizontal cross, tight-set where the two strands intersect. Then, starting at an inward point, a perfect circle is woven, and concentric ones from this outer circle in. The noiseless patient spider perfects each round, each areally smaller than the last. The open bullseye at the center is shrunk to a point, but not completely erased. There's about a half-inch between the innermost circle and the center, where the spider stations herself to sit, watch, and wait. As sun behind pines lowers, changing air temperature generates winds that toss this architecture, frolic assaults. It is ultimately unmoved. Truths the spiders know.

1854—**Walden** *published*

Sinking Creek Journal

August 10   **HEAT THERAPY**

Days of unremitting heat, clear sky. One would think the cultivars would wilt, but they hold out, as though the heat were a form of therapy for water addiction. In fact, grassed areas too low and easily waterlogged now grow more swiftly while golf courses and medians and close-cropped lawns brown. Tomatoes flourish in their pots, okra on baking terraces, beans in their flower niche bloom blue. Even the gerbera daisy has a new purple flower. The wild fields out there, the wild tinted-window drivers on the roads, seem untouched. In fact, to whatever extent this drought and heat-wave is tied to "global warming," the human and non-human natural communities, for better or worse, seem unaffected on the ground where they live. Only the news anchors show concern.

> "*—as lovers*
> *who are walking on a freezing day*
> *touch icy cheek to icy cheek,*
> *kiss, then shudder to discover*
> *the heat waiting inside their mouths.*"
>   Galway Kinnell, "The Perch"

August 11   **POLLINATION**

Black-winged damselfly rests on gourd vine far from water. This vine is impressive. Last year's dried-out predecessor seeded it, now its refulgent orange five-point starflowers, filled with honeybees, fan out as the vine crawls its erratic way over the parking space, its journey its destination. Already its fruit swells, green and yellow or all yellow, not yet big enough to display the bulb shape and ridged surfaces. Much less successful are its close relatives the pumpkins uphill, striving outward, bigger stars but no bees and no fruit. What is wrong with the pumpkins' advertising campaign? Maybe they simply lack conviction, commitment, and the pollinators can sense this. Perhaps the scarlet runner beans, with long furry green pods already, and the gourds, both raised from homegrown seed, are like free-range chickens, smaller but more integrated into their environment.

*1922—National Coast Anti-Pollution League
founded (Gifford Pinchot president)*

August 12   **RAGWEED TOLERANCE**

    The ragweed is in bloom. Of course its flowers are green and unobtrusive, yet it takes dominion everywhere, like nothing else in Tennessee. And nowhere is that dominion more absolute than by Sinking Creek. Its towering hempy stalks return no matter how completely they seem to have been uprooted before pollination the previous year. They colonize, control, yearn for monocultural dominance. You just have to live with ragweed, clear it repeatedly where it most threatens your little darlings, but not waste energy on a dream of extirpation. So much in nature demands tolerance from humans, so much do they overextend trying to deny it. We were born into discomfort, its absence is just a bright hibiscus flower, a one-day perfect bloom.

1896—Gold discovered on the Klondike River

August 13   **JES SITTIN**

Sittin aside of the road them speedin cars come at you like to make you meat a-hangin off your own mailbox if they fails to make that little curve adjustment in time

Sittin aside of the road them vines look to circle yer neck and flower in yer ears

Sittin aside of the road the creek's dried itself into silence

Sittin aside of the road by phlox seedpods brownin all summer hang like potater chips when will they fall

Sittin aside of the road swallertails an skippers cruise it drivin u.i. but safer than yer 4 X 4

Sittin aside of the road cicada music seems wingin high above like tree wall's own self singin

Sittin aside of the road sun thread godalmighty sycamore limbs an heat rise an fall on my boozed-up skin

Sinking Creek Journal

1954—Multiple Surface Use Mining Act passed

August 14   **UNWATERED**

Thunders split to the north and south last night, leaving us marooned on our island of drought. Further south it must be even worse. On this treed island dew clings every morning and must provide some moisture since uncivilized and unwatered things stay green, for example the ironweed, full royal purple now, wingstem more than seven feet tall. Moist enough for puffball season to return—one so far, already aged to green with brown patches. Tomatoes flourish, must be trimmed again, purple morning-glories peer over guard rails, heavy gravel-laden trucks rumble incessantly to and from excavated fields.

1933—Tillamook Burn forest fire in Oregon (to September 5)

August 15   **KNOWING TOO MUCH**

Two more days of 90s, they say. The butterfly weed seedpods bear clustered orange/black sucking beetles, thick like pomegranate seeds. Sprayed off, in a few hours they're back, thicker than ever, at distance colorful enough to be flowerheads themselves. Makes one consider from what unpleasant knowledge the limits of perception protect humans. Seems so many "advances" of human knowledge necessitate thinning this ozone layer of security, from Van Leeuwenhoek's microorganisms in sputum to global warming's plankton extinction cascade. The more we know the more we know the fateful consequences of our knowing.

"There is no defense against an open heart and a supple body in dialogue with wildness." Terry Tempest Williams, **An Unspoken Hunger** (1994)

August 16   **BUTTERFLY POLITICS**

Butterflies perform maneuvers, appropriately, around the butterfly bush. Often, as everywhere, it's an interspecies ballet, like bird feeder display.

Here the smaller green swallowtail is jousting with the spicebush swallowtail. The first descends upon the second, who rises from her feeding, dances briefly, again is teased, rises again. The tiger swallowtails, larger and more numerous, maintain by contrast an aloof, businesslike demeanor, fluttering systematically among stalks. Occasionally a red admiral skips over the roof, observing swallowtail mania with a hint of skepticism. It isn't only other butterflies that receive such treatment. Border collies *aplatis* in the shade garden are romanced by blue skippers dancing at their muzzles in a mode of incitement hard to accept as accidental—roused, the collies snap and grunt. In August butterflies and their progeny rule: beneath foliage the human needn't wait long for some brilliantly paletted furry caterpillar to arrive from above and begin to explore an open palm . . .

1916—Migratory Bird Treaty between the U.S. and Canada

August 17   **MANTIS**

Creekbed almost completely dry. Unusual cloudy morning. Yellow leaves on franklinia. Startled—so effective its camouflage—by four-inch praying mantis, fully clothed—dry leaf, stick color. Hose spray disturbs her, the lightning predator awkward stalking grass to find new elevation. Mantids can eat hummingbirds (not to mention mice), and the hummingbird feeder was put out yesterday. They graze the same terrain. Our mantis is an import, the Oriental mantis (*tenodera aridifolia sinensis*) and an unembarrassed cannibal. She can rotate her head 180° and misses nothing. Her attraction for humans may well reside in the anthropomorphism of her posture—one could call her behavior inhuman. One would certainly like to believe her ethics are not shared by *homo sapiens*.

1947—Mineral Leasing Act for Acquired Lands signed

August 18   **CRICKETING**

Now late afternoon before cicadas, field crickets chatter, just above the tinnitus level, a field of sound, a swift and steady compression of airwaves. Sinking Creek has died, scum entropically dots the bridge's stagnant pool.

Sinking Creek Journal

Kiss the fish goodbye—a strange thought. But the crickets sound activity, plump blackly on stone circles or at flower stems, seem to thrive *en masse* where the ground is hottest. You can hear the crickets knowing what the season is, where their place is in the world at large, how soon they will be husks.

> "...only the cricket will be up,
> repeating its one shrill note
> to the rotten boards of the porch,
> to the rusted screens, to the air, to the
> rimless dark . . ."
> Mark Strand, "My Mother on an
> Evening in Late Summer"

August 19 — Spatial Con

But if this chronicle seems entomologically dominated recently, that's only because nature in these latter days is similarly dominated. The grass spider, for example, in the last week has established her trampoline web in the front raised bed, right across the May-night salvia. Unlike last August's orb-weaver, dancing upon a complex verticality, the grass spider spread a vibrant, nonadhesive mat that curls sloping down to a hidden funnel amid thick, fleshy sedum stems. The spider's own plateau of flowerheads, still green, provides a perfect shelter and hunting blind, and drought minimizes need for web repair. Above the spider's mat is a proscenium barrier between phlox. Flying food impacts this vertical web, falls disoriented onto the mat, to be paralyzed and hauled down the funnel. Clearly, larger (more intelligent?) insects recognize this sophisticated spatial con. The syrphid fly grazes all around it, even on the may night salvia itself, never touching the springe, perhaps, by human analogy, respectful of another species's craft.

> "Without Insects, there would be no spiders, and without spiders there would probably be too many insects."
> Gilbert Waldbauer, **What Good Are Bugs?** (2003)

August 20   **WITHER?**

    Trees, unlike humans, endemically conserve energy. In a drought like this one, they close down and bring on an anachronistic fall, a fall of dead colors. Our trees have mainly not reached that point yet. Around here, it's mainly acanthus and, unfortunately, maple, that wither among the green. How strange that these living things "lower" on the intelligence scale, have a greater wisdom than those on high. The Earth is drought-stricken, and the human machine grinds on toward oblivion.

"Sometimes there is no leaving, no looking westward for another promised land. We have to nail our shoes to the kitchen floor and unload the burden of our heart. We have to set to the task of repairing the damage done by and to us." Janisse Ray, **Ecology of a Cracker Childhood** (1999)

August 21   **BAT TIME**

    Not usually out here this late. Tree masses black, sky pewter. Corpse of heat overlays the valley; bats are out, erratic black flutter and swoop; above them, swifts' precision curves and return, like the skillful cutting of grey fabric. There used to be more bats, feasting at the streetlights. One July 4, fireworks in light drizzle drew bugs, moisture weighted them down, legions of bats fluttered, gorged among Roman candles.

    No one seems to have inhabited the bat house on a sycamore down by the creek. But maybe we have just been observing it at the wrong time. Human time and bat time don't coincide.

"Most of the time he hangs quite still . . . He seems content, dormant again, as if withdrawn into a dream of death. On the floor next to the stove the cat sleeps, curled away from him, and only I am mindful of either, or myself." Robert Finch, **Death of a Hornet** (2000)

August 22   **SPECIES AT HOME**

    Monarch caterpillars at last, not on milkweed but on the butterfly weed they share with those aphidic orange beetles. Will there be enough to feed them all without killing the plant? Fortunately, there's rue next door, healthy blooming yellow, and they've been seen on it in years past. Yet to see a completed green chrysalis. There are other true aphids, on sunflower leaves, shepherded by ants, a common interspecies relationship, sort of like that between border collies and sheep. The mantis is still here also, pretending to be a woody stem of rue. She's clearly claimed this crib. Don't most life forms possess that "sense of place" oft claimed by ecohumans as their exclusive attribute?

"Far more creatures than is generally realized show attachment for a home territory and in it some special site." Lorus and Margery Milne, **Paths Across the Earth** (1958)

August 23   STAPH

Thinking of the human body as environment, the artifice of its sustenance, like a garden in a bottle, the artifice of survival in a world of suffering, a bubble on the surface of a deoxygenated pond. At the same time the opposite of artifice: microorganisms are infinitely less herdable than cats. First world hospitals crawl with staphlococci. If every living creature invisible to the human eye could suddenly be seen, humans would have no antibiotic to fight the fatal consciousness of this reality.

"William Marcus had been let go by the tannery after 38 years of work, without a pension. He also happened to be dying from a rare form of lymphoma." Jonathan Harr, **A Civil Action** (1995)

August 24   ALTERNATIVE REALITY

Now, two showers later, Sinking Creek is a byzantine trickle between stones, framed, nay, buried, in heaping jewelweed bushes—orange on our side, rarer yellow on the other. All summer these wet waste spaces have nurtured its imperceptible green growth. Now its fulness creates the illusion of an alternative reality to the drought: the jewelweed blooms dance as the hummingbird taps them, and gold wild sunflowers and dogwood berries swelling, elderberries already ripe and black, okraflowers unfurling pink, the goldfinches bungeeing flowerheads.

1992—Hurricane Andrew devastates Florida

August 25   **MEAGER**

Pokeberries begin to darken too, hang in orderly bunches, a claim to legitimacy. Small purple gentian entangles edgerows. Heat-exhausted cucumber tree, yellowing fast, can't know rain is on its way. Sparse okra pods fatten anyway, are meagerly harvested, as are the last curvaceous Japanese eggplant fruit, snipped off withering plants. Undaunted, the gourd vines grow daily, their bumpy fruits bump against the bumpers of Erick's parked truck, surround it in a pulpy embrace. Gnarly untended turnips, unfit for cultivated society, are tossed. The highway dust is really over all.

1859—"Colonel" Drake strikes oil at Titusville, Pennsylvania

August 26   **REDEEMED SPACE**

The drought has broken with evening downpour and silver flashes between branches. Dan has mowed the dry dry grass into blowing chaff, but rain has mulched it down. Fresh scents rise from the earth, leaves fill out. The franklinia has lost its yellow and set forth one waxy white bloom, on which a skipper perches. Flow into pools has strengthened. The basil buds must be plucked or they will all run to seed, and now their sweetly metallic scent o'erspreads redeemed space . . .

1909—First convention of the National Conservation Congress

August 27   **INDIGENOUS STONE**

Beautiful terrains of living stone creekflow, fresh but low enough to sandal up, snail-slipping, clutching roots. Some creek stones are composition, or edgeless bricks, but mainly they're a watercarved indigenous menagerie, each shaped as though for a definite, mysterious purpose: here's a flat brown disc, scarcely irregular, quarter-sized, imaginary pre-Columbian currency. Particularly attractive are the extreme, elongated rectangles and cylinders—how could sheer water force create them? Collies slosh, Tam Lin hops rock to rock, everyone loves the creek now; erotogenic reek, we clamber the riprap, now it's flat, bright, level, mown, while down there, the undecoded truths.

"The actual stones in the world are not symbols of permanence so much as they are temporary landmarks or bookmarks. They are reminders of a continuing dialogue between humanity and the natural world . . ." John Elder, **Pilgrimage to Villombrosa** (2006)

August 28   **PLEBEIAN FEAST**

Although there is a sedum society, hundreds of species under cultivation, sedum has its detractors. Its outcurved fat stems, fleshy leaves, broccoliesque blooms can spread widely, sagging back over other plantings, a concealing ugliness. But sedum has such unusual and late-blooming flowers, they ignite the end of summer, however overbearing; and after all, you merely need string corsets to contain them. Their heads seem to have two general forms—either broad cones, or flat plateaux which the winged kind can employ as aircraft carriers are. This is the season when the massive heads of tiny buds first break into color—subtly differing roseate and orange tones—and are first invaded by gangs, usually insects and the smaller butterflies. It is a plebeian feast. Here brown elfin butterflies, less than an inch long, crowd the surface as though all born of the same litter, mixed with diverse smaller bees and wasps. The grass spider, wise to this new development, has spread her trampoline more widely, beneath the crowd, anticipating fatal appetites.

2005—Hurricane Katrina reaches Category 5; no evacuation order

August 29   **FLATS**

Up in Cherry Hill community, past the well drillers and the miniature horse farm, Embreeville flats spread out, the dark green mountain steeps retreat, the brokebacked red barns close in, with browning cornfields beyond. The wild fields here are all sunflower and joepyeweed, roadkill flourishes—fawn and possums, the latter sharp teeth and open mouths, almost as to say "well, I expected it." Cattle-crowded stream, deep under sycamores Little Joe's Auto Salvage scattered meagerly with grass-swallowed bodies, one rusted Bel Air, all wheels present yet displayed on blocks. Even out here one finds the occasional many-towered mansion on a rise, dominating trailers, sheds, dead farm machinery. All is corn or desiccated pasture or high grade green foothills except, closer to town where they begin, the magnolias are brown-mottled green as if they can't decide . . .

2005—*Hurricane Katrina makes landfall*

August 30   **FATAL POOL**

Despite it all, the creekflow sustains, even if only a trickle, even unto this penultimate day of August, and with it, the two pools deep and aerated enough to preserve trout and other minor minnows. One trout under the bridge is eight to twelve inches long. Seems like only a rainbow (an introduced species) could survive the water temperature of this hot summer; through the misty green filtered water it appears to have a side streak as it silkily plies amid the mossy stones and disappears when sensing a human watcher's shadow. Although the Tennessee Appalachians preserve 625 miles of trout streams, most are to the east, at higher and colder elevations. The trouts' provenance is mysterious; there has been no water flow full enough to carry even fertilized roe from the heights down here into the shadow of suburbia. With other dry months ahead, they seem to be in a fatal pool . . .

"I both respect and pity the brook trout. On the one hand, a stream-dwelling population of native brookies elicits admiration, even reverence . . . [but] . . . Painful to say, they seem to be losing the evolutionary battle." George Constanz, **Hollows, Peepers, and Highlanders: an Appalachian Mountain Ecology** (1994)

Sinking Creek Journal

August 31   **INTIMACY AND EXHAUSTION**

Very tiny inchworm—more a quarter-inch worm—inches over a check about to be written. The inchworm on the check, omenous. Franklinian? Spend in measure? Prudence? Measure for measure? And then the spider beside the coffeemaker—entrapment in caffeine addiction? Lots of creatures are getting very close: yellow jackets wreathe the head, suspended hummingbirds stare meaningfully through the picture window, swallowtails brush the face. What is this febrile communication? The sun is glazed, weary. *En masse*, summer is wearing out; *en particulier*, it seems to be heating up.

"As much as I love the firm grasp and cerebral order of Spring, there's a ripe, almost sensual pleasure in its August abandonment too." Michael Pollan, **The Botany of Desire** (2001)

September 1   **DOGWOODS**

The dogwoods' first red berries are on show, along with the hibiscus's last bright red flowers. It seems the color comes first to the dogwoods' most sun-exposed branches. . .the ripe berries are the perfect harvest for birds before temperatures fall (if indeed this year they ever will). Our three dogwoods have cycled healthily here year after year, more than a quarter century, despite the constant threat of leaf cover. Enforcing sun exposure is vital to them, as their survival is vital, since this same period has seen great dogwood decimation from anthracnose, a fungus that takes its greatest toll on shaded trees. The property has seen its plagues of non-fatal anthracnose; some years a fruit tree or flowering bush will have its leaves wholly blackened, but somehow these dogwoods have avoided even this temporary fate.

1914—*Martha, the last passenger pigeon, dies in Cincinnati*

September 2   **JUST ANOTHER DAY**

Coolest morning in months—dew almost chilly on legs. Moths flee desultorily, only a few bumblebees graze. Air seems full of spiderwebs with no visible means of support. Vague horsetail clouds scarcely drifting. Rising sun, crows and their neighbors caw, jays honk, collies pant and observe bright-eyed the swelling light. Brown elfins begin to land on the sedum, Tam Lin observes chickadees with mild interest. To humans of a certain persuasion it's Sunday, to the rest of nature just another day.

> "How long ago the day is
> When at last I look at it . . ."
> W.S. Merwin, "Any Time"

September 3   **SEASONAL DIFFERENCES**

Been to the friends in their former pasture subdivision, north side of town. The "25 Acres Zoned RP3" sign still dominates the surviving pasture, as we approach. It is hotter here, drier, most properties lightly treed. The friends' tomatoes and Mediterranean herbs are thriving. Across the shallow valley, dotted with luxury homes, brown excavated hilltop still holds out. Talk turns to seasonal differences, places of origin: in Newfoundland it has snowed by the end of September . . . turns again to blurring of these differences: never saw so little snow as last winter. Thinking everything is always all right at any particular point in time, as now, but the more points are summoned up, the bleaker dips the line of nature's health.

> 1964—Congress creates the National Wilderness
> Preservation System (Wilderness Act)

September 4   **ST. JOHN'S WORT**

Our St. John's wort is not *hypericum perforatum*, the species most touted for its psychoactive effects, but one of the 400 other *hyperici*, one particularly developed as an ornamental herb, but not one of the half-dozen native to Appalachia. It seems to resemble most closely *hypericum canariensae*, native to the Canary Islands. What distinguishes ours is that only now has it started to bloom. All summer its long, reaching, close-leaved stems have extended, and we have continually thought it was wanting to flower. Now, in September, white small blooms are springing from each

Sinking Creek Journal

leaf bract all along the stem, like tiny pussy willow cushions; soon each stem will be a wand, just in time to conjure up late summer warmth.

1886—Geronimo surrenders to Gen. Nelson Miles

September 5   **METAMORPHOSIS**

We noticed the chrysalis yesterday, hanging by its slender nub underneath a sedum bloom. It didn't seem like a monarch's: stubby in shape, dark aquamarine, and a thin white horizontal line around its widest circumference. This afternoon, peering in, no chrysalis. Then it materializes, milky, empty—and beside it a full-sized monarch butterfly, its head alone seeming the size of the chrysalis, wings stiff; occasionally it fans them, waits, as though coming to terms internally with its metamorphosis and the brave new world opened to it. It waits, and as in a pre-thought instant, rises, flaps, glides in figure-8s and donuts. Then, as though from the exhaustion of unaccustomed movement, it lights on the boxwood. A new lightness has entered the worn world.

1881—Thumb Fire in Michigan destroys a million acres and kills 282

September 6   **GARBAGE AND PREDATION**

Long time since we all went up the woods trail—not a great deal seems altered. Earth is dry, foliage dusty, a skim of brown newfallen leaves. Alpine and blue-stemmed goldenrod (the latter's blooms all along each stem) are challenging the drought, along with white asters like baby daisies. Human impact is here also: there's new garbage in the dump, track-spanning fallen logs have been sawed up, and wheel-gouges head downward. But most notable are the spiderwebs. At this sun-angled hour they're filled with light, lines across the trail, black lumps their dangling denizens, the tangles in every low plant. The train is a veritable cafeteria, the lines are long. Garbage and predation, alive and well.

"We saw more carp, more muskrats, mudflats covered with sandpipers, and the frozen-in-time remains of a snapping turtle that appeared

to have been decapitated by a train. We also saw a thermos, three unopened cans of pepsi . . . and a Seven Seas Red Wine Vinegar Salad Dressing Spill." Robert Sullivan, **The Meadowlands** *(1998)*

September 7   **RELICS?**

    The only change: logs blocking the trail to wheeled access sawed and shifted. The cleanline sawmarks, sawdust piles, we must be able to get there, no roadless area for us. All the rest of the forest is the same only dustier, even the shaved homestead, except for cover of born and dying grass—the stagnant pond—maybe just a hiccup, never to be humanized again, only regrown, reclaimed, half-remembered patch in time, relicized as rusted-out loggers' rails poking like ribs from between tree roots.

"My album is the earth, and the pictures in it are faded and badly torn and have to be pieced together by detective work."
Loren Eiseley, **The Night Country** *(1956)*

September 8   **HARVEST FLY**

    This morning on hose by brick housewall for warmth, green cicada, big head, transparent stained glass wings, magnificent name "dogday harvest fly" (*tibicen canicularis*). When enlivened by dog day's heat it will call "like a circular saw cutting through a board." Pokey now, easily moved to a leaf, maybe seeing fate in cooler nights despite sweltering days, an emblem maybe, strong coda, putting period to this overbearing time for humans and other species that cannot die conveniently soon or hide underground in disguise but must forage on in thrall.

1900—Galveston hurricane kills 6,000

September 9   **BENDING**

    Time of bending stems—ironweed, wingstem, goldenrod, ragweed, the last in bloom but strategically topheavy, big bend outward where the terrain is clear, like the heavy imperial stride, so the eventual seeds will fall on

Sinking Creek Journal

fresh ground, tribal territory will grow. The bending falling stem so assertive with irony, like High John the Conqueror bowing with a wink to the lash ... and up front, around the bridge, are just-blooming future benders, the golden asters, compact sunflowers, tall, thin-leaved, bright-faced, waiting their turn.

> ". . .we smile too in welcome back
> To all the joy and anguish of
> The earth we walk on, lie down in."
> Robert Penn Warren, "Diver"

September 10   **CASH HOLLOW**

Downhill from the Higher Ground Holiness Church is one tail end of TVA Boone Lake, fishing shacks, spindly docks—afar off, expansive water, first crouching McMansions, baroque toads. All in weekday afternoon daze. The TVA lakes sprawl, many-armed, mutant cancer cells, shaped by the creek and river beds they drowned. Down the other way from this high point, Cash Hollow Road struggles through a network, stream-carved coves that might have, save the jiggle of a 1930s planner's pen, been engorged themselves, themselves hosting baroque toads. The only cash in Cash Hollow is probably generated by oxycontin. "Dangerous Curves:" dense tree cover opening to skinned-trailer compounds, trashpiles, mutilated cars, tent sheltering piles of dead glass, tracks to blasted barns and subsidiary dead-end hollows. All the same—a planned community of dysfunction, generations old, its own integrity the moldy scent of hopeless sufficiency.

> "A little lower, on the plateau where our house sits, a spiderweb of old fenced wires is stuck to the ground by different kinds of barbs. Livestock once lived here. Someone tried to make a living from this land."
> Chris Bolgiano, **Living in the Appalachian Forest** (2002)

September 11   **SPIRIT OF CHANGE**

Before sunrise the sky is misty blue, air is still, awaiting. By noon, wind whips pearly gusts, pinprick droplets, like an oceanside breeze without the salt. Humans move and talk more quickly, or linger outside in the drizzle, agitated, enervated. This coolness has been so long gone, it affects like a fountain in the desert. Gusts strengthen, a mixed yet sparse rain, a different drummer on the skylight. Sunflower body language nods and bobs, while the imperturbable cat awaits the impossibly foolish bird in a dogwood leafdance. Undeniably some spirit of change is traversing these mountains, a *nuntius*, a forerunner, a herald in cape of gold.

1961—World Wildlife Fund founded

September 12   **LEAF DANCE**

Ginger remarks on that certain September slant of light, so inexpressible, as though all phenomena were illuminated at a slant from earth, beneath, in figure the curve of a wave just *after* its crest. The great pin oak seems, in its unending rivalry with sibling sycamore, to want to participate in this observation: a light blow to the leg, an acorn fallen almost in the lap, a wakeup fall, an announcement. Then, at the end of a single spiderweb strand from the oak's branches, at least twenty feet long, there's one tiny oak leaf, windblown, the low sun hits it perfectly, it dances, dances, frenetic twirls, midair possessed, a sparkle, captures attention to death, dances Time away.

"I prefer to embark from the shore on the questionable security of an air mattress. I feel a pleasant identification with the environment when being blown about like a leaf on a world as old as time."
Ann Zwinger, **Beyond the Aspen Grove** (1981)

September 13   **COUCH IN THE FOREST**

Sittin' on a couch in the dump, between blooming white snakeroot and rusted oil drum full of bullet holes, reflecting on the limits of rhetorical ecocentrism. In fact, there's a whole living room suite out here, whose dark and ghastly plaid would be unspeakable between walls, but which blends perfectly with the forest's dark browns and greens. Thinking how the human voice intrudes its humanness by very definition, however well-disguised as "nature," like a couch in the forest, forest where every view of every space has a couch in the center, a pop-up ad, a floater in the eye. When an authentically ecocentric narrative could be told, for example, only by a tree in the language of leaves.

1977—First U.S. diesel automobiles produced by General Motors

September 14   **DAYS DWINDLE DOWN**

Rain steady all day, but light, tentative. Doves fight unconcerned, soggy sunflower husks, squirrels hang like pelts on walls, sucking seeds. Monarch in high flight cruises between droplets, poises, pulsing wings, disguised as a yellowing dogwood leaf. At every drop, Mexican sunflower leaves bob, vibrate, eccentric equatorial jangle, while other plants hang stoic and absorb. Withering down of days: single blue/yellow hidden aster, single white cabbage butterfly, black spot pinned on. Darkening landscape, every window still green. Trying summer: late freeze, endless drought. Yet life abundant nonetheless.

> *"Summer means promises fulfilled, objectives gained, hopes realized . . . Then one day, lying on a path, there is a tiny leaf of aspen, bright yellow with a border of red along the veins. This is a sign and I look at it with disbelief. It cannot be true, it is far too early . . ."*
> Sigurd Olson and Les Blacklock, **The Hidden Forest** (1969)

September 15   **ABSENCES**

Morn chill and dark. Scarcely enough rain for a trickle down the creek. Minnows flip silver in shallow doomed pool. Watered butterfly bush now glorious purple-plumed, but its clients all hidden or deceased. Crow calls. Lemongrass fountain spills over. Age-raddled plant pots. Collies, damp, unmotivated, grunt. A single bumblebee. The apple tree is sterile. It is all an expressionist mood, a truly pathetic fallacy. Hummingbird and goldfinch dance in pear leaves. Crows increasing, conference call. Box turtle wet and shiny, head out, unconcerned. Where are the suns of yesterday?

1835—Darwin's Beagle reaches the Galapagos

September 16 **CHILL MORNING**

    Pignut, snakeroot, goldenrod, chill morning, barkful, lots of trailscent pauses. A bearshaped upended tree root. Up top the homestead's grass bowl Faye scares a young whitetail—two—in chase they veer upright, bounding, pure air velocity versus collie's lowdown determined flashsprint, in her element, the voyage itself her destination, while Leif, secretly lazy, immerses himself in the mudpond. Sun rises, vision is crystal, particulates grounded. Now the cat alone is sneezing. It's molting time, they say. The cardinals are patchwork-clothed, the birds need nourishment, refeathering in the cold, just as the deflowered sunflower seedheads become ripe. Something is done right.

1987—Montreal Protocol on ozone depletion signed

September 17 **SUBDUED**

    Last of the last, blue asters bloom, droop long stems over the necks of the aging jewelweed. There are 68 species of asters in the Appalachians. Here the local variety adds another layer to the foliage that crowds and shrouds bog and streamlet. So irrigated by seepage, all remains lush and pungent, while the hillside, drier, scents sharp of straw as the tall latesummer flowers fade leaving their heads exposed. Occasional premonitory leaves fall; okra, now head high in grass, does still bloom, as do the sterile pumpkin vines. A single small scarlet-thorax dragonfly poises, its color shrieks in the subdued field. Whir of hummingbirds.

1930—Construction of Hoover Dam begins

September 18 **THIRST FOR PURPOSE**

    Rising sun focused through precise declivities resembles a flashlight beam, changing objects with the moving eye. Is there a purpose in this track-lighting, a schedule, a sequence of illuminated dark-surrounded stumps, junipers, dogs? Intentionality, human consciousness, radiates out, stored with half-recalled primitive observatories, Hobbit scenes, astroglyphs. Thirst for purpose in a dry forest. And then the shredded windfalls

Sinking Creek Journal

all along the trail, all clawed and fragmented, one even in the very middle, not there two days ago—the collies sniff obsessively. They've been very attuned these days; the evening bark continues long after sunset. One has to suspect a natural explanation: black bears nearby, grubbing for winter, inhaling dormant pupal protein itself waiting in the soft wood. It's time to watch out for birdseed and garbage raiders, the foraging brotherhood.

> "With that first turtle I crossed a boundary of greater dimensions than I can ever fully comprehend. I changed lives within a life, worlds within a world . . . Turtle was the alphabet of a new language, and not only a passkey into a new world but a key to open the gate of a world I knew I had to leave." David M. Carroll, **Self-Portrait with Turtles** (2004)

September 19   **DRY NIGHT LIFE**

Cygnus centers the sky this September night, the swan, symbol of migrations south. Vega in Lyra alone among stars withstands light pollution. Other bright stars waver in their trajectories, are revealed as satellites. The waxing moon through foliage mirrors the neighbors' spotlight glare. Air is soft and crickets chant endless harmony. Only Faye enjoys wandering the landscape, years' habitude directing footfalls, ground mapped by touch. Drought has a distinctive scent, not unpleasant, more like the dryrush fragrance of pleached flowers in a vase. This afternoon hawks, red-tailed probably, passed though, crow-jeered. They know infinitely more this night where'ere they perch about dry night life than any sense-bound human exalting in a recognition of stars.

1844—Marquette Iron Range discovered, Michigan Upper Peninsula

September 20   **SHOOTING GALLERY**

Pickup on the gravelled track. Below the cleared homestead and pond dam, facing uphill, is a dude on treestand, camouflage gear, netting over face, hostile tone: "What're you doing?" "Walking my dogs." "You got permission?" "I've been walking my dogs here for twenty-five years." "This's my land. You need permission. Get off it." The thought: "Well, will you give me permission?" But not to be cocky with an armed man. "Yup." The collies appear to have understood, head downhill unusually fast. Unclear sight: did he have bow or rifle? TWRA bow season for deer begins September 22, gunning not till November. The scales have fallen: this entire setup—grass, pond, saltblocks—this whole space is but an elaborate funnelled shooting gallery for deer. What would Farmer Bastian think? Down with tradition, up with property rights. New year close, new route to find. End of an era.

> *"Crawling in the duff, I bring my head slowly over some exposed tree roots and see elk before me, around me, moving everywhere, big dark shapes in the trees . . . I raise the rifle, wanting to fire, but also wanting to wait."*
> Ted Kerasote, **Blood Ties: Nature, Culture, and the Hunt** (1993)

September 21   **GENOCIDE UNDER GLASS**

Washing windows is a disconcerting task. An untouched summer has filled their embrasures with desiccated insects, tattered webs of deceased spiders—"Irish Lace"—but also with innumerable egg cases, they hang like clumps of fruit. Spiders, thoughtless of approaching genocide, still guard many of them. There are hatcheries over sills and in corners. It is a challenge to brush them down without destruction, a challenge to pretend not to see those still clutching their cases in corners and not wipe them down. There's another conflict here, for why does the human need clear glass between the sheltered self and reality, why any barrier at all, why any dwelling, even?—and then this quandary is so abstract and self-righteous. Why does the spider need the window? At least to keep the window, let its offal accrete. If you need clear vision, step outdoors. Scraping off gummed feathers, remembering the cardinal impacting, bouncing off stunned, the redtail in seconds taloning it, rising, cleaning out a victim.

> *"Deanna stood at the edge of the porch and raised the paper from the lid of the cup, giving the cup a gentle heave to send the moth on its way. It tumbled and struggled in the bright air, then swerved upward for several seconds, grasping at sudden freedom. A phoebe darted out from the eaves and snapped the moth out of the air. In a vivid brown dash she was gone again, off to feed her nestlings."* Barbara Kingsolver, **Prodigal Summer** (2000)

September 22   **THIRST**

The vulture of evening caresses a too-blue sky. Gold distils through branches. High winds whip drought-stricken trees, the crackle and chaff flies. Exhausted sunflowers bow. It feels like a sandstorm without the sand. The molting towhee, a sorry sight, dances. The times are changing. Shivers of expectancy. Gnarly gourds torn up before they rot fill a bowl. They have a savage look. All the dogwoods prematurely yellowing, monarchs have fled, one solitary fritillary humps a Mexican sunflower. Creation is athirst.

"On my way down the canyon, I stopped several times to wade in the creek. I watched little black trout who lived and breathed in it, but I fought, nobly I judged, not to take a drink of it myself. I tried to think of various things, but by the time I was half way down the canyon I could think of nothing but drinking." Norman Maclean, **A River Runs Through It** *(1976)*

September 23   **HOW SWIFT THE JOURNEY**

Fallen off a cliff from summer, only a few rain dashes but cool now, shady canyon time, far off the sizzling plain. How swift has the journey been across this unit of terrestrial time filtered through a human consciousness. The foliage clings yellowing, but there are no banked postcard maple leaves. White asters do signal, but goldenrod is dry and parched on the staff, snakeroot withers. No doubt it will rain again, tunes again will strike up the old dance of mortality. "Keep them wanting more," says nature, we all do, on this we can all agree.

"But the stream of time moves forward and mankind moves with it . . . Yours is a grave and a sobering responsibility, but it is also a shining opportunity. Therein lies our hope and our destiny. 'In today already walks tomorrow.'" Rachel Carson, *"Of Man and the Stream of Time (1962)*

About the Author

Fred Waage grew up in Ithaca, NY and graduated from Princeton University with a B.A. and Ph.D. (1965, 1971) in French and English. He taught English at Northwestern University at the height of student rebellion (1968–71), and then went to California, becoming one of the many folks whose lives were changed there. He was a Junior Research Associate at the Huntington Library, taught at Cal State, LA, got divorced, was an assistant manager at Jack-in-the-Box (fast food) in Pasadena, was temporarily brainwashed by the Unification Church (the Moonies), living a few blocks away from where the SLA kidnapped Patty Hearst.

Most importantly, he escaped the cult and was hired by the environmental organization Friends of the Earth, based in San Francisco, which had recently been founded by famous environmentalist David Brower after he was fired as director of the Sierra Club. There he became acquainted with people, issues, and places of environmental significance in the vibrant years following the first Earth Day.

When by fate or fortune he ended up back in academia and in New Jersey, he was thinking of ways to bring environmental concerns into the college humanities curriculum. He briefly and futilely self-published a little magazine named *Second Growth: Literature of Environmental Concern*. More importantly, he married his former creative writing student, Ginger Renner, collected unemployment, got hired for one year at College Misericordia (now University) and they lived coldly on a frozen lake in the Northern Appalachians.

Fred and Ginger (go ahead and laugh) were saved from the cold (1978) by East Tennessee State University, in Johnson City, where they have lived ever since, not on a lake but on a freshwater stream, the living source of this book. There they have raised generations of border collies and their son Erick (a 1st Lieutenant and West Point graduate) and Melissa (Princeton, '01, of the Natural Resources Defense Council).

Fred was the founding editor of the significant Appalachian magazine *Now and Then*. He has published books on Renaissance dramatists Thomas Dekker and John Webster, and papers on the same literary period, but his greatest interest as a teacher is environmental literature and writing. He has published poetry, fiction, and creative nonfiction on nature in chapbooks and periodicals. He edited a groundbreaking text, *Teaching Environmental Literature* (1985), one of the inspirations for the environmental literature movement begun in the 1980's, and embodied in the Association for the Study of Literature and Environment. He coedited (2008) the radically expanded edition of *TEL*, *Teaching North American Environmental Literature*. He has written a literary biography of American environmental writer George R. Stewart, and is completing an ecocritical study of much neglected novelist Ross Lockridge's *Raintree County*.

Semper fi

Coming Soon to the
Little Creek Bookstore

Eating Local in Virginia
Phyllis Gross

Take a tour across Virginia's bountiful farmlands and meet many of the organic food and goods producers from around the state. Go to www.littlecreekbooks.com for more information.

To see all of the Little Creek Book titles, or to purchase additional copies of SINKING CREEK JOURNAL, signed by the author, visit our website:

www.littlecreekbooks.com

Little Creek Books

A division of Mountain Girl Press
Bristol, VA